"This book represents the culmination of Rita Gross's many years of serious practice, reflection, academic study, and scholarship. Rita really dug in! Here she generously shares her innermost thoughts, passions, and struggles in what has become the last memoir of one fiercely dedicated to the Buddhist women's movement."

—ELIZABETH MATTIS NAMGYEL, author of
The Power of an Open Question and *The Logic of Faith*

"In this final book, Rita M. Gross's insights into both the Buddha's classical teachings on identification, self and no-self, and the present-day challenges of gender roles in Western Buddhism shine through. Useful to Buddhist practitioners, students of gender roles in religion, those working for gender equality, and anyone interested in the process of Buddhism's assimilation in the West, *Buddhism beyond Gender* contains thought-provoking material to further any discussion of these."

—SHARON SALZBERG, author of
Lovingkindness and *Real Love*

BUDDHISM BEYOND GENDER

LIBERATION FROM ATTACHMENT TO IDENTITY

RITA M. GROSS

INTRODUCTION BY JUDITH SIMMER-BROWN

SHAMBHALA
Boulder
2018

Shambhala Publications, Inc.
4720 Walnut Street
Boulder, Colorado 80301
www.shambhala.com

9 8 7 6 5 4 3 2 1

First Edition
Printed in the United States of America

♾ This edition is printed on acid-free paper that meets the
American National Standards Institute Z39.48 Standard.
♻ This book was printed on 30% postconsumer recycled paper.
For more information please visit www.shambhala.com.
Distributed in the United States by Penguin Random House LLC
and in Canada by Random House of Canada Ltd

Designed by Kate E. White

Library of Congress Cataloging-in-Publication Data
Names: Gross, Rita M., author.
Title: Buddhism beyond gender: liberation from attachment to identity /
Rita M. Gross; introduction by Judith Simmer-Brown.
Description: First Edition. | Boulder: Shambhala, 2018. | Includes
bibliographical references and index.
Identifiers: LCCN 2017020818 | ISBN 9781611802375 (pbk.: alk. paper)
Subjects: LCSH: Women in Buddhism. | Sex role—Religious aspects—
Buddhism. | Identity (Psychology)—Religious aspects—Buddhism.
Classification: LCC BQ4570.W6 G7625 2018 | DDC 294.3081—dc23
LC record available at https://lccn.loc.gov/2017020818

CONTENTS

PUBLISHER'S NOTE

Shambhala Publications is honored to be publishing Rita Gross's final book, *Buddhism beyond Gender*, which she completed shortly before she died. The draft she left behind contained a few unfinished sections. She had included a placeholder for a discussion of transgender issues, and she also intended to add material on Tara as well as stories from Mahayana sutras. While she was never able to contribute these remaining sections to the manuscript, her last work offers a compelling and thought-provoking exploration of the suffering caused by clinging to gender identity—indeed, to any identity at all—and how we might liberate ourselves from this prison. Her manuscript was edited with care to remain true to her original intentions for the book.

INTRODUCTION

JUDITH SIMMER-BROWN

This book is a beautiful final gift from the pioneering Buddhist feminist and teacher Rita Gross—you might say her last testament. Rita was writing this book at the time of her death from a massive stroke on November 11, 2015. She was in her beloved home in Eau Claire, Wisconsin, accompanied by her Siamese cats, her five hundred houseplants, her delicious library of scholarly, religious, and spiritual classics, and her many Buddhist artifacts, statues, and paintings. Writing was her passion; she had already completed six books and edited five more; her published articles are numerous. But it was always her dream to publish a dharma book with Shambhala Publications, and this one represents the pinnacle of her offerings. Rita was a close friend and colleague, and it is a great honor to introduce this book to you.

Rita came to Buddhism after a tumultuous history with religious communities. Raised in the German Lutheran Church in northern Wisconsin, she was excommunicated at age twenty-one for her edgy inquisitiveness and independence. In her first marriage, she converted to Judaism briefly and continued to appreciate Jewish ritual and communalism, even while she chafed at its patriarchal structures. India beckoned her with a pantheon of dynamic goddesses, and she entered a lifelong love affair with Hinduism, but she avoided institutional involvement. In 1976, she moved to Boulder, Colorado, and Naropa Institute to explore her attraction to Buddhism and meditation, and that is where she finally found a spiritual home. Sitting practice became a peaceful refuge; study under the tent of Tibetan Buddhism fed her voracious intellect; and guru devotion stole her heart. She became a student of Chögyam Trungpa

Rinpoche, and entered the demanding training of the Shambhala Buddhist tradition.

When Rita became a Buddhist, however, she came with a fresh "outsider-analyst" perspective.[1] She was a feminist scholar and had cofounded the 1971 Women's Caucus of the American Academy of Religion. As one of the few female graduate students at the Divinity School of the University of Chicago in the 1960s, she had dared to insist that the religious experience of half of humanity was ignored in the study of religion, and she completed the first dissertation in the emergent field of women's studies on the topic of Australian female aborigine religious life. Her male professors were constantly taken aback by her clarity, persistence, and boldness in forging new methodologies in the study of religion, ones that relied on women's voices—personal narrative, biography, lay ritual enactment, and anthropological case study. She shared these innovations with her feminist colleagues, and a new field of women's studies was born.[2]

Given her history with patriarchal biases in religious communities, she entered her newfound Buddhist community with caution and critique. As she wrote, "Having already had trips through two sexist religions—Christianity and Judaism—I had no interest in repeating that experience. Enough already with patriarchal religious institutions!"[3] Later she wrote of how deeply Buddhism spoke to her, explaining that she could not avoid becoming a Buddhist. "Buddhism was simply too profound to let the patriarchs have it without protest," she later wrote.[4]

As Rita and I became friends in that Shambhala Buddhist community in early 1978, we shared a passion for feminism, for meditation, and for liberative Buddhist teachings. I also had experienced the crushing effect of patriarchy in academia and society, and I also struggled to reconcile a spiritual hunger and a feminist thirst, to borrow terminology from the feminist author Carol Flinders.[5] As Rita and I completed long retreats together, the longest one lasting three months in the spring of 1980, we both felt the power of practice to settle the mind, open the heart, and refine the intellect. This led to deep conversations and many questions that laid the basis of lifelong friendship.

By 1985, Rita and I hatched a plan to write a book together, and we proposed to the State University of New York Press a feminist critique of Buddhism (hers) and a Buddhist critique of feminism (mine). She had previously edited two books of essays, *Beyond Androcentrism* (1977) and the groundbreaking *Unspoken Worlds: Women's Religious Lives* (1980), the first collection of case studies about women from disparate cultures. I had published only a few articles and was an unknown in the publishing world. I deeply appreciated Rita's generosity in suggesting this joint project. We negotiated a contract and began our work.

As we developed our outline, we encountered the differences that would ultimately lead to dissolving this particular book partnership. Rita felt a stronger affinity and trust for feminist perspective, and she sharply criticized in the finest detail the patriarchal structures of Buddhist texts, traditional institutions, Tibetan monasticism, American Buddhist communities, and Shambhala Buddhism itself. Even as she felt unquestioning devotion for our mutual teacher, Chögyam Trungpa Rinpoche, she could clearly see the circle of men who surrounded him and ran his organization, and she saw the obstacles faced by women who stepped at least temporarily into positions of power.

I shared these perspectives, but I was personally so inspired by the practice, the liberative teachings themselves, and the experience of belonging to a close-knit community that I was willing to navigate the injustice. In retrospect, I realize that I had arrived in Boulder as a student of Trungpa Rinpoche as a refugee from searing experiences on the feminist battleground, probably more intense than Rita had directly experienced. Or perhaps I was not as tough as she was. I had suffered the indignities of a Human Rights Commission class-action suit against my university, and its backlash, when they terminated me without cause. After my termination, I had directed a rape crisis center for three years, during which I had served as an advocate for sexual assault victims in hospitals and courtrooms, while encountering their imprisoned rapists in experimental confrontation interventions. While these experiences were in some way empowering to my feminist sensibilities, they were also personally and emotionally devastating. I was spiritually hungry. Applying myself to the rigorous demands of practice, study, and service brought tremendous healing and liberation. I recognized that feminism would not address my deepest suffering, and I sought a spirituality that would.

As Rita went on to write her 1993 landmark book, *Buddhism after Patriarchy,* her "metamorphosis from outsider-analyst to insider critic and advocate"[6] became manifest. In this book, she took what she called "the prophetic voice."[7] Following women's studies and feminist methodology, she intricately untangled the threads of Buddhist traditions that could support a feminist practicing within a historically patriarchal tradition. She valorized the liberative teachings of Buddhism while assailing the patriarchal structures that thwarted the ability of those teachings to genuinely deliver women's liberation. In so doing, she addressed with clarity and consistency Buddhism's ambivalence toward women.

At their foundations, the teachings of the Buddha clearly were aimed equally at the liberation of both men and women. Rita demonstrated that teaching after teaching in the Buddha's sutras of the early period, as well as in the Mahayana, assured liberation for women, speaking of women's enlightened potential, their capacity for practice, and their commitment to awakening. Surveying the foundational Indian teachings, Rita self-consciously "revalorized" Buddhism, meaning that she determined that no matter how sexist Buddhist institutions might appear, the tradition as a whole is not irreparably sexist.[8] The purpose of her book, she wrote, was to retrieve "an accurate and usable past" that feminist practitioners could rely on as they committed to Buddhist practice.[9]

Nevertheless, human-made patriarchal structures from Indian society permeated Buddhism, so that female monastics were relegated to lower status, women played little role in leadership, and educational and meditative training was denied them. This follows a pattern of patriarchal religion everywhere, Rita argued, and suggests that Buddhism as a religion has denied the very foundations the Buddha intended. For this reason, Buddhism requires a "feminist reconstruction" in order to fulfill its promise embedded in the foundational teachings.

In her extensive critique and reconstruction, Rita distinguished between the foundational liberative view and the institutional conservatism of Buddhism, and her reconstruction envisioned what she called a "two-sexed" model of a vital, creative spiritual tradition. She called this "androgynous" Buddhism, in which women and men cocreate a living tradition together. Rita challenged women and men to free themselves from the "prison of gender roles," her very definition of feminism. Until her death, she was committed to androgynous Buddhism at tremendous risk to her academic career and reputation.

Rita was well known in feminist circles in religion for her critiques of patriarchy and androcentrism, but many in Western and Asian Buddhist communities do not know the impact in those circles of her groundbreaking work. Shortly after the publication of *Buddhism after Patriarchy*, I was a presenter at a conference at the University of Toronto on the wide-ranging impact of the book. The feminist presenters there ferociously attacked Rita for practicing and advocating for a hopelessly patriarchal religion. The Buddha was male, they argued, and the patriarchal structures of Buddhism reflected his own biases. They detailed many of Buddhism's sexist sins, real and imagined. How in good conscience could a card-carrying feminist like her betray her convictions so drastically?

In spite of this rejection by her previous feminist colleagues, Rita became the spokeswoman of a Buddhist feminism in the decades to follow, traveling North America and the world on behalf of disenfranchised women. She was renowned among Asian Buddhist women for her advocacy, and she spoke frequently at dharma centers of the major practice lineages in North America. For decades, she was a regular presenter at conferences of Sakyadhita, the international Buddhist women's organization that advocates for Buddhist nuns and for leadership roles and education for Buddhist women worldwide. Eventually Rita herself moved into more centralized leadership roles within Buddhist institutions, first as a senior teacher and meditation instructor in Shambhala International and then later as *lopon*, empowered teacher, representing Her Eminence Jetsun Khandro Rinpoche, leader of the Mindrolling lineage of Nyingma Tibetan Buddhism in the West and a rare woman *tulku* incarnation. Until her death, Rita taught courses and led retreats at Khandro Rinpoche's primary meditation center in the Shenandoah Valley of Virginia. This was the most fulfilling and joyful period of her life as she nurtured dharma students and guided them in their study and practice. Rita adored Khandro Rinpoche and faithfully practiced the teachings of the Nyingma as a pillar of her Western lineage.

What began as solitary advocacy from the margins matured for Rita into leadership from within. Her later books bring Buddhist feminism into the mainstream of contemporary Western Buddhism, and her 2009 book, *A Garland of Feminist Reflections*, represents a retrospective of her forty years of explorations.[10] Her activist voice changes into that of an elder thinking back over her years of challenging boundaries. She writes of her hesitancy to focus so much on her intellectual work and writing on feminism and women's studies, saying it all had a "certain accidental and reluctant quality."[11] But given the rampant androcentrism and patriarchy of academia and the world, this work was necessary for her full functioning as a complete human being—she was compelled by what she calls "circumstances and necessity."[12]

In previous books, Rita's prophetic voice awakened Buddhists to the necessity of completing dharmic endeavors, drawing from the core liberative teachings of the Buddha and critiquing androcentric institutional structures in order to open positions of leadership, authority, and learning to Buddhist women. In this current book she moves to another endeavor—supporting those same Buddhist women to sink into dharma teachings in order to fully find their own liberation from the prison of gender roles. She does this as senior dharma teacher, pastoral in her view and wise in her detailed counsel. In reading, we know she has tread this path herself and is showing us how to find the deep spiritual food we have hungered for. She has come full circle.

In this book she chides contemporary Western women and men for their excessive attachment to gender and for the gender stereotypes they hold that imprison themselves and others. She argues that clinging to gender roles has caused immeasurable suffering for women and men, and she observes that an essential point of the path is to contemplate the egolessness—indeed emptiness—of truly existent gender.

Yet the path Rita lays out is not mere spiritual bypassing. That is, it is not helpful to just assume that gender is meaningless or inconsequential and that mind beyond gender is accessed through some kind of leap of faith. She warns us that finding freedom requires deep training and precise contemplation, denying neither the absolute nor the relative truths along the way. Her book is a classic study of the Noble Truths through the lens of gender identity.

The first chapters of her book describe again, summarizing many of her previous writings, how both female and male gender roles are imprisoning for Buddhist practitioners, the first Noble Truth. Women have limited access to teachings and practice opportunities. They are expected in traditional societies to prioritize caring for their husbands and families and are warned away from independence. Their bodies are challenged with menstruation, pregnancy, childbirth, and child-rearing. They also are demeaned by male projections upon them as sexual objects. In societies that place a premium on appearance, old age is a direct threat to women's status. Men also are imprisoned by gender roles, which include the expectation of their economic, cultural, sexual, and physical success. Men suffer also from fears of being feminized in a culture where this is considered denigrating. Rita speculates that the male gender role may actually be killing men. The purpose of this portion of her book is to inspire a classic Buddhist desire for renunciation, couched within gender roles in our everyday life.

The cause for this suffering is that women and men have unthinkingly clung to their gender identities, Rita argues. Feminists can be just as guilty of this clinging as others in focusing excessively on their female identities. This clinging leads to fixation on victimization as well as to arrogance regarding female birth. It also causes the suffering of others, as when feminists disrespect nonfeminists or men. She reminds us that releasing clinging is the key to relief from suffering from the prison of gender roles and suggests the use of classic Buddhist practices to do so. Ethically, we need to commit to doing no harm and to refraining from sexual misconduct. This will bring tremendous liberation, she promises.

What does freedom from the prison of gender roles look like? she asks. Again, she turns to classic Buddhism. This freedom is not so much about changing lifestyles to traditional or radical ones; it is about changing the mind. The enlightened mind has equanimity but is not apathetic. The enlightened mind still sees injustice, patriarchy, and androcentrism. Not relying on anger, the enlightened mind moves to challenge these and change them. She argues that Buddhism has always had a feminist thread that opposed male dominance and that feminism has been indigenous to Buddhism.

Along the way, she challenges socially engaged Buddhism to take up the cause of feminism, as she wonders why this has been so lacking in Buddhist activism.

There are moments when we might wonder if Rita had not quite finished her writing. She tended to work alone on her books, and I had never seen this manuscript until her passing. If I had seen it earlier, these are the questions I would have asked:

Rita, what more could you say about critiques of the gender binary itself that imprisons not only women and men but also those who do not identify with either? Could you address transgender practitioners? (Shambhala editors informed me that Rita had, in fact, intended to include a short section on this topic, but it was never completed.)

What perspectives might you develop about intersectionality, an analysis of the interlocking oppressions that create societally imbued prisons of race, ethnicity, class, ableism, and ageism? You know that third-wave feminism acknowledges that women come from a variety of sociocultural locations—black, brown, queer, poor, non–English speaking. Surely there is more to this endeavor than understanding the constructed nature of gender alone and being included in Buddhist institutions? Isn't the prison about more than gender roles?

Rita, could you provide more explicit examples of studying the constructed nature of gender identities along the classic lines of Madhyamaka logics or Mahayana emptiness contemplations? Your book begins with Dogen Zenji's injunction that to study the Buddhaway is to study the self, and that to study the self is to forget the self. Could you trace more closely how we study the self so that we could forget the self?

All in all, this book clearly gathers Rita's many years of thinking, writing, meditating, and teaching into one flowing narrative, sharing from a dharmic perspective how we can free ourselves from clinging to gender roles. Finally, this is what she cared about most, and this was most central to her own journey from liberal and then radical feminist to senior Buddhist teacher and feminist elder. It is a fitting culmination of a lifetime of sparkling analysis, dogged determination, and heartfelt devotion to the liberative path of dharma.

Judith Simmer-Brown is Distinguished Professor of Contemplative and Religious Studies at Naropa University in Boulder, Colorado, and Acharya in the Shambhala Buddhist lineage of Chögyam Trungpa Rinpoche and Sakyong Mipham Rinpoche. Rita wrote of her: "Judith has been my closest and most long-term Buddhist friend all these years. . . . She is the only person with whom I share so many of my passions—feminism, the world of Buddhadharma, interreligious exchange, and academia. . . . To those four concerns we could probably add a mutual love of India."[13] Judith's book, originally planned with Rita, is *Dakini's Warm Breath: The Feminine Principle in Tibetan Buddhism* (Shambhala Publications, 2001). She has also coedited, with Fran Grace, *Meditation and the Classroom: Contemplative Pedagogy for Religious Studies* (State University of New York Press, 2011).

BUDDHISM
BEYOND
GENDER

ONE

BUDDHISM AS STUDYING THE SELF AND FORGETTING THE SELF

The great Japanese teacher Dogen Zenji wrote that to study the Buddhaway is to study the self, and that to study the self is to forget the self. These inspiring words accurately describe what is the problem with clinging to gender identity or any other form of identity and how to overcome that problem. Buddhism is a spiritual discipline for studying the self so that it can be forgotten. It might sound as if forgetting the self along with any problematic aspects of one's identity is the solution, but how can one forget the self? Only by studying it. Thus, to understand how clinging to gender identity subverts enlightenment, it will be necessary to study gender both as it has been discussed in Buddhist discourse and practice and as worldly conventions have constructed it.

I was being introduced at a Vipassana center to give a talk I had titled "How Clinging to Gender Identity Subverts Enlightenment." This is a talk I give frequently. The voice and facial expression of the center's highly regarded guiding teacher communicated confusion and dismay as he told the audience that I would be talking about "how gender subverts enlightenment." I had to interrupt him: "No, it's how *clinging* to *gender identity* subverts enlightenment." The operative word is "clinging" not "gender."

On another occasion, I gave the same talk at the Rigpa Center in Amsterdam. After I finished the talk, one of the men in the audience approached me. He said he had found my talk challenging, but it had not challenged him at all as a man (a male human); the challenge had been to his Buddhist understanding and realization. He realized that his understanding of the core Buddhist teachings on egolessness, the lack of a permanent, enduring, unitary identity, was still weak. It was weak because he still identified quite strongly with contingent, ephemeral dimensions of his experience as if they were substantial and real. He also realized that it was irrelevant that those ephemeral elements of his identity happened to be connected with his masculinity. The same would apply to women and their clinging to conventional notions of what it means to be female. It also applies to any other identity, sexual, national, cultural, or religious, which people take to be of overriding importance, clinging to it as if it mattered ultimately or as if it were a reality, rather than an appearance. What was relevant was the extent to which he still relied on those ephemeral factors to define himself, taking them to be much more important and real than they are—the quintessential mistake that subverts enlightenment. He then said, quite passionately, that it would be helpful if I could write a short book on what I had talked about. That is to say, he was asking me to write a basic dharma book but to apply common terms like "clinging" and "egolessness" to topics like sex and gender.

When people, including Buddhists, think about sex and gender, they usually ignore standard dharma, relying instead on worldly conventions. At a talk I once gave, one audience member actually claimed that because sex and gender appeared very plainly to her and have a biological basis, they had to be truly real, to really exist, and to be determinative. Confusing appearances for reality is common even among Buddhists who are well educated in Buddhism. This confusion is at the heart of all the suffering we inadvertently bring down upon ourselves.

DISMANTLING CLINGING

The dharma is so simple and so basic, communicated in the second of the Noble Truths. Suffering is not random, inexplicable, nor caused by an external agent. It is the result of clinging, grasping, fixation—one of the many words that could translate *trishna*, of which "addiction" may be the most adequate modern translation. Yet it seems to take immense amounts of practice and contemplation to get the basic point. Phenomena, things, are *not* the problem. The problem is *what we do with* those phenomena, taking them to be much more real than they are or can be, in the case of gender becoming so attached to conventions surrounding sex and gender that we turn them into a *prison of gender roles* to which we cling, which produces suffering and subverts enlightenment. Conventionally, we make sexual or gender identity into a real, permanently enduring self, the kind of ego or self that Buddhism has always denied.

Short of teachings by the Buddha himself, I know of no text or teaching that more clearly captures what we need to do to proceed further in this puzzle of how to rid ourselves of clinging to gender identity and being locked into the prison of gender roles than the writings of Dogen Zenji, the great thirteenth-century teacher so closely linked with the foundations of Soto Zen Buddhism. In the *Shobo Genzo* he explains,

> To study the way of enlightenment is to study the self. To study the self is to forget the self. To forget the self is to be actualized by myriad things. When actualized by myriad things, your body and mind as well as the bodies and minds of others drop away. No trace of enlightenment remains, and this no-trace continues endlessly.[1]

The operative phrase here is that "to study the way of enlightenment is to study the self." Then, after, only *after* we have *studied* the self, can we *forget* the self. If we try to forget the self before we have thoroughly studied it, we will only ignore or repress it. Buddhist teachings are clear that repressed aspects of the self always come back to destroy us. The Buddhist curricula of all schools of Buddhism are also clear and definite. One always studies how the phenomenal world works in order to know how to transcend it, how not to be imprisoned by it. In a progressive curriculum of Buddhadharma, one first studies *skandhas, ayatanas, dhatus,* and *nidanas* and tries to find a self in them.[2] Then one asks over and over: Does the mind have color, any racial color, any gender shape, and so forth? Is it inside the body or outside it? "Find it, find it!"—find that essence of yourself that you posit and think is so real!—is the insistent demand of Buddhist teachers. Only after thoroughly exhausting that search, and finding no relative identity that meets the standard of being ultimate and enduring, can one rest in the peace of egolessness. Thus, not being done in by any identity, gender or otherwise, thereby subverting our own enlightenment, is a matter of both *studying* and *forgetting* the self. Both are necessary. To be able to forget something, a great deal of study or contemplation is often first required.

Egolessness is a fundamental Buddhist teaching. It would be hard to locate a more basic teaching. But it is also a steep teaching. People are often incredulous when they first hear of it. I once sat for the oral defense of her PhD thesis by a graduate student who had written about engaged Buddhism and social issues. One member of her committee was an expert in religious studies from a related field but knew little about Buddhism. When the candidate, I, and others on the committee routinely talked about egolessness and how it pertained to her thesis, that committee member wanted to halt the proceedings because he felt the assertion of egolessness, that there is no permanent identity or self, had to be wrong, which would have invalidated her whole thesis. As the ranking Buddhist scholar-practitioner on the committee, I had to tell this person that, in no uncertain terms, he was out of order, that egolessness is a well-established Buddhist teaching and we simply were not going to debate its validity.

Buddhists, on average, do a little better, though once when I was teaching a weeks-long course for intermediate students at a residential meditation center, I encountered a student who was mystified and shocked when the topic of egolessness came up in a survey of core teachings. He simply refused to believe that it could be part of Buddhadharma, even though he was in a course whose purpose was to prepare students to begin Vajrayana, or Tibetan Buddhist, preliminary practices. I asked how he had gotten to this point in his commitment to Buddhadharma without having come to terms with teachings on egolessness. He replied that at the major urban center he attended, the topic had come up in one course he had taken, but he decided the idea was so far-fetched that he would ignore it.

However, unless they are very new, most students claim to believe in egolessness because that's what they've been taught. But they can't really explain those teaching to their friends and relatives, which means they don't yet thoroughly understand them. The Buddhist ignorance is to imagine that certain treasured aspects of our relative identities can go with us into the egoless state of enlightenment. Or to imagine that some treasured aspect of our relative existence actually has ultimate, unalterable permanent relevance. Gender ranks high on that list. Many people, both women and men, simply cannot imagine what they might be without their specific gender markers and traits. Nor do they know how to relate to a person who does not exhibit strong, clear gender markers; they become confused and defensive, turning away if they can. Early during second-wave feminism, in the 1970s and 1980s, stories circulated of people who clothed their infants in yellow. Other people refused to interact with those "ungendered" infants because they had no idea how to relate with a human being except as a male or a female, even when that human being was a mere infant. Humanity disappeared into gender, as so frequently happens in conventional, samsaric interactions. Once when I was teaching at a weekend-long program on Buddhism and gender at another urban meditation center, a sweet young man commented at the end of the program, "Without my moustache and genitals, I'd have no idea who I am!" I wanted to shout, "Bingo! You've got it! Stay there, holding conventional gender markers very lightly."

Which is it going to be? Clinging to gender identity (or any other identity) or attaining enlightenment? In the early scriptures preserved in the Pali language, the Buddha often told students to investigate thoroughly whatever aspects of their conventional lives they identified with, that they felt were their own, that they thought were important, reliable, enduring. If they persisted in their investigations, they found that whatever they identified with as their own, or as who they were, could not rise to the standard of being an enduring, reliable identity or self. And only by going beyond all these identifiable, graspable anchors could true freedom be found. The same kind of language persists unbroken in Buddhist traditions all the way through to contemporary teachings of Theravada forest traditions, Zen masters, Mahamudra, and Dzogchen. The third of the Noble Truths clearly and definitively describes what the cessation of suffering entails: "It is the remainderless fading away and cessation of that very same craving, the giving up and relinquishing of it, freedom from it, nonreliance on it."[3]

WHY GO BEYOND GENDER?

What "it" has a greater hold on people's imaginations or limits them more than ideas about what biological sex must mean, what I call "the prison of gender roles"? Almost all conventional people—often called "ordinary worldlings" in Buddhist texts—as well as many Buddhists hold fast to the notion that sex and gender *must* mean something definitive and incontrovertible. I cannot count the number of times convinced, sincere Buddhists who believe in egolessness have, nevertheless, adamantly argued with me that gender could not be dharmically irrelevant. It felt so real to them, the most real factor among their many identities, and, therefore, must *mean something*. In fact, a well-known Buddhist author once asked me to write an essay on what is distinctive about women's enlightenment experience! I declined that invitation but countered that I would contribute an essay called "How Clinging to Gender Identity Subverts Enlightenment."[4] To imagine there could be something distinctive about women's enlightenment experience is to suppose that gender identity exists as a real entity, rather than as something ephemeral and ultimately insubstantial. It would entail the claim that gender identity, alone among conditioned phenomena, is not empty of inherent existence but truly exists. Clinging to gender identity and letting conventional ideas about gender dictate one's life thus contradicts all central Buddhist teachings. One would then also have to contend that egolessness is gendered, which would be a self-contradictory, illogical proposition. Imagine trying to hold on to both ends of the contradiction: *though there is no permanent abiding self (or ego), nevertheless gender is real.* Illogical as that proposition is, many seem to hold to it nevertheless.

Why, if it is so absurd to regard egolessness as gendered and if clinging to gender identity indeed subverts enlightenment, does the prison of gender roles remain so strong? In Buddhist terms, such errors of judgment usually result from insufficient analysis and contemplation, and will persist so long as serious analysis and contemplation are lacking. And no one, least of all the Buddha, ever said it would be easy or quick to do the analyses and contemplations required to *fully realize the relative character* of all our relative, samsaric, worldly identities, to stop expecting more of them than they can possibly deliver. Nevertheless, that transforming and transcending change of expectations, no matter how difficult it may be, is what we need to accomplish if we want to be free. I once heard a wise Buddhist teacher say that if we could realize what the Buddha had understood in an hour or two, even a year or two, or possibly even a decade or two, it probably wouldn't be worth much. But no one who has ever experienced some taste of freedom from the conventional, including freedom from the prison of gender roles, has ever said that it was not worth the requisite time and discipline.

Buddhist disciplines need to include contemplation of these truths and the development of greater awareness of them. Yet mere mention of feminism, gender, women's equality, or related topics brings giggles, hostility, and an assumption that such discussions could be of interest only to women and need not concern men, even though men are as fully gendered as women. These common ways of rejecting those who bring up topics pertaining to gender give the impression that the proper dharmic response to questions about gender is to ignore and suppress them. Especially when teachers are answering questions from timid (usually female) students about gender and Buddhism, a usual response is to strongly suggest that only people who are not sufficiently dedicated to Buddhadharma would ever think of raising questions about traditional Buddhist ways of dealing with gender—that good practitioners would not raise such issues.

Countless times I have heard revered teachers reply, somewhat angrily, to questioners, "Aren't you over that yet!" or "Don't you know than enlightened mind is beyond gender, neither male nor female, so, therefore, concerns about gender are unnecessary and irrelevant?" The Asian teacher newly arrived in the West says in a shocked voice, "But in Asia, we really revere our mothers." Or the quintessential answer of the inexperienced teacher, "Just practice more. Sitting on the cushion solves everything. Eventually you won't mind gender discrimination if you just practice enough." No other dharmic question generates the answer that it would be more dharmic to just ignore what gives rise to the question!

The deep pain buried in these questions about gender deserves better answers than telling students that they should have already transcended that pain when they have only begun to have a little awareness of the peace that transcending conventional, samsaric ego can bring. And the teachers need to explore far more deeply how much the suffering of the samsaric ego is intertwined with the gendered ego—for both women and men. In fact, we should equate all three terms and use them interchangeably—"conventional," "samsaric," and "gendered" ego.

But when dharma teachers answer questions about gender in such fashions, their very defensiveness, which turns so quickly into a recommendation to ignore, indicates that they may not have fully come to terms with the questions themselves. Asian teachers dealing with Western students may be misled by the superficial, recent veneer of equality between men and women, assuming equality to be much more deep-seated in the West than it is. For one thing, Western students have never been taught that "enlightened mind is beyond gender, neither male nor female." Nothing in the Western religious or cultural heritage even hints at a state of mind "beyond gender, neither male nor female." Everything from the original human being to the deity is sexed—male sexed. Everything of value in the culture has been the monopoly of males. So how could a Western student be expected to take as a real possibility for herself what the Buddhist teacher expects her to already know? It seems to me that some Asian teachers have little intimation of how much their Western students have internalized Western stereotypes of female inferiority and how deeply they have been scarred by their religious upbringing. Additionally, few male Asian teachers have worked deeply with female dharma students in their cultures of origin.

Contrary to all the revered teachers who recommend that, because enlightened mind is beyond gender, we should ignore our discomfort with conventional, deeply entrenched practices surrounding gender, Dogen Zenji's text tells us we *must* study that gendered self before we can truly forget it. And, that if we do not study the self, we can't and won't forget the self either. Clearly, this sequence of studying and then forgetting applies to the gendered self as much as to any aspect of the self. It is curious that traditional analyses using "color" or "shape" to break down our assumption of real selfhood never use the terms "male" or "female" in the same way. This omission allows people to easily believe in egolessness while clinging to conventional gender norms and stereotypes. Would it not be just as useful to disclaim selfhood based on having a male or female form as it is to disclaim selfhood conferred by color or shape? Doing so intensifies the deconstructive power of analysis, making egolessness much less a theoretical belief and much more an "in your face" reality. Without that additional step, people can easily do the traditional exercises and genuinely believe in egolessness but still be quite attached to gender.

But if we all believe that enlightened mind, the natural state of mind, is beyond gender, why is it important to so rigorously deconstruct gender? When teachers scold students who bring up gender issues by reciting the slogan that enlightenment is beyond gender, they are missing an important point. People cannot go to a state of mind "beyond gender" on the spot any more than they can just drop self-grasping the first time they hear teachings about egolessness, even if they immediately and intuitively grasp the truth of those teachings. That transformation takes a great deal of time and effort, and just as training is necessary for people to actually approach egolessness, so is training required to transcend the prison of gender roles—which, in fact, amounts to the *same thing* as relaxing into egolessness. Neither just happens. Additionally, a large percentage of self-grasping is not just ego-grasping. It is grasping at an ego that is deeply conditioned by its residence in a male body or a female body, and for many people the maleness or femaleness of that body takes precedence over its humanity. It is important to grab people where they really live, which for many is with their gender assignments. Until those attachments are cut, there will be ego-clinging, no matter how much people may believe in egolessness. Giving absolute answers to questions about the relative is unskillful in the short run, even if such answers are true in the long run. Instead, we must follow Dogen Zenji's advice and first engage in thorough study of the gendered self, probing its reality and significance deeply. It is pointless and naive to claim that we can study that self without studying its gendered aspects, even though generations of Buddhist teachers may have done so.

TWO

IDENTITY, EGOLESSNESS, AND ENLIGHTENMENT

At one point, I entertained the possibility of titling this book *How Clinging to (Gender) Identity Subverts Enlightenment*. I wanted the parentheses to emphasize that while gender identity and the prison of gender roles are main concerns of mine, those concerns are embedded in the whole matter of identity and how much we absolutize and cling to various identities. It was decided that such a title was too confusing and cumbersome. But from the dharmic point of view, identity, not gender, is the main topic of this book. This is because gender identity is one kind of identity, and clinging to one's identity, sometimes called "identity view," is a major problem according to Buddhism. We have already seen that "forgetting the self" is at the heart of Buddhism. Because people are often confused about the meaning of egolessness, it must be stated again that teachings on egolessness do not deny the everyday sense of having a self or being someone. One's identity clearly *appears* and is important in a non-ultimate way. What is denied is the reality of the self, its permanence and ultimacy. These limits apply to any identity: national, religious, cultural, or gendered.

People who do not belong to a dominant group (male, white, heterosexual, and so on) are often accused of being too aware of their identities, as in "playing the race [or class, or gender] card" when they point out that people with their identities often do not receive equal treatment with people who belong to "majority" identities. By contrast, while those in dominant groups may acknowledge some of their identities, such as "American" or "Christian" they are often in denial about the advantages their dominant identities bring them. Some people may claim that they don't have an accent "because all the radio announcers talk like I do," or they might not be aware that they are also limited by cultural assumptions. They just don't want to admit that everyone has an accent and a culture, even if it is the dominant identity. People who are male, white, or heterosexual often claim that they are un-affected by those identities, that they are simply "normal" people. Regarding gender, this is especially the case. Frequently, men do not regard being male as belonging to a specific gender. Their as-sumption is that women are gendered, but not them, an assump-tion that their behaviors often reveal. I have often found this out when I give talks on "gender." The audience is usually well more than half women, which should not be the case, given that every-one, not just women, belongs to some gender. I have also been accused of "genderizing the dharma" because I frequently discuss gender differentials in Buddhism. I can only respond: I didn't do it! I'm only pointing out what's clearly in the Buddhist texts and Buddhist records. If that information makes you uncomfortable, perhaps you should look inward a little more deeply, but please stop blaming the messenger for a message you'd rather not have to deal with.

In any case, according to basic Buddhist teachings, no one of any identity is exempt from the implications of teachings about egolessness and the downside of clinging to identity. That applies, of course, to a feminist identity, though I have run into some fem-inists, newly converted to their identity, who believe that their newfound identity is of superior value or validity to other iden-tities. This is somewhat like the always-failed attempt to find an ideology, a creed, or a version of history that is "really true," unlike everyone else's. But the point of this book is that clinging to iden-tity subverts enlightenment; gender identity just happens to be an identity that is often embraced without any awareness that it is an identity or that one is both clinging to it and reaping the benefits of that identity. Those comments certainly apply in droves to male identity.

SEXUAL SEGREGATION AND IDENTITY

Before a baby is out of the birth canal, in many cases well before then, a sexual identity is slapped onto it, and with the sexual identity also a gender identity and the prison of gender roles that accompanies it. These labels depend only on external biological markers that indicate that in the future this child will produce either sperm or eggs. They tell us nothing about the child's IQ, its karmic possibilities, its abilities, interests, or potential. Everything about this baby, and every other baby, is trumped by the sexual identity forced upon it. In many societies, including most traditional Buddhist societies, the child is introduced to a world in which men and women are treated almost as if they belong to two different species having two completely different sets of roles and interests. Sexual dimorphism is emphasized to an extreme degree, and common humanity is lost in gender segregation. Sexual segregation is intense, and women and men meet each other primarily to have sex and reproduce. In that sexual segregation, the cultural activities valued most highly, including most learning and most spiritual practice, are off limits to women, deemed to be appropriate only for men, while women are made to be servants and enablers of men.

This sexual segregation is justified by claiming that women distract men who are trying to concentrate on important affairs and that sexual misconduct will soon follow if men and women mix more freely. To these claims I have often responded that if the only occasions on which men and women are allowed to interact are somehow a prelude to sexual intercourse, then, of course, men and women will distract each other, but if they learn to carry on important activities in each other's presence they soon learn to interact as human beings, not merely as potential sexual partners. As for the claim, commonly made, that women must be kept invisible and protected in a private realm because "men cannot control themselves" in the face of sexual temptation, I have often wondered why men should be given control of the world if they cannot even control themselves sexually. To the common solution for an epidemic of rape—keep women sequestered—why not sequester the men instead, given that they, not women, are the rapists? Yet in society after society, in one way or another, women pay the price for men's uncontrolled sexual appetites.

That so many react to this lethal cocktail of extreme sexual dimorphism, enforced heteronormativity, and male privilege by developing alternative gender identities such as feminist women, profeminist men, or any of the gender identities covered in the initialism LGBT—lesbian, gay, bisexual, and transgender—should not be surprising. These alternate identities often provide a sense of relief to those for whom the conventional gender arrangements simply don't work. We live in an era of "identity politics" in which many oppressed and marginalized groups—not only those who do not find conventional gender arrangements compelling, but many other groups—have found their voices and are insisting upon being treated with dignity, respect, and equality, and on having the freedom to be themselves.

From any Buddhist point of view, it seems to me, such developments must be regarded positively, for Buddhist institutions have done their fair share of harm by conceding to conventional social arrangements and oppressive hierarchies that have little in common with the cardinal Buddhist value of compassion. Yet identity politics also have their limits from a dharmic point of view. If absolutized and clung to, as identities often are, they entrap one in further suffering as readily as does any other relative, contingent composite that is clung to. However important liberation from the pain caused by social injustice may be, it is not the ultimate liberation that Buddhism envisions. Looking into social injustice and working for freedom from it can be an important part of "studying the self," but it is not yet "forgetting the self," to refer to Dogen Zenji's pithy comment once more. While many people would undoubtedly suffer less in a world free of patriarchy, heteronormativity, and extreme sexual dimorphism, that world would still involve the suffering brought about by attachments, especially the confusion of self-centeredness and ego-clinging that plagues all who have not truly "forgotten the self." Concern with "identity" is hardly distinguishable from "ego" or self-cherishing, understood in Buddhism as one of the four things we are most likely to become attached to, thereby keeping ourselves caught in a trap of disappointment and frustration.[1] According to Buddhism and to any simple contemplation of our own experiences of longing and disappointment, desires and attachments never yield complete satisfaction and peace; they always disappoint in the long run. Is there any pain worse than the pain of wanting things to be different than they are in the present? But they could not be different than they are, due to causes and conditions already in place. Recognizing that one's pain is actually caused by one's insatiable longing brings immediate relief. That is the peace of "forgetting the self," even the feminist self, the gay or lesbian self, or the transgender self, a peace that is of another order. This does not mean that those relative projects are unimportant but only that they cannot and do nothing to bring the peace of "forgetting the self."

BEYOND IDENTITY IN ABSOLUTE AND RELATIVE TERMS

When we try to ascertain the relationship between teachers' claims that we need not worry about conventional gender arrangements because enlightened mind is beyond gender, neither male nor female, and Buddhist institutional male dominance, we run headlong into the puzzle of the relationship between the two truths, absolute and relative. Buddhists have long insisted that trying to reduce everything into one absolute truth is unworkable. There is a nonconceptual *absolute* truth that remains forever uncapturable in a verbal, discursive formula, though it is experienceable in space and silence, and discursive, *relative* truths for handling the myriad phenomena we encounter in daily experience. Buddhists always say, however, that these two truths are inseparable and that balancing them is one of the most difficult tasks of an adequate spiritual life.

In terms of gender, absolute truth pertains to the ultimate irrelevance of gender, its conditioned and relative character, a point agreed upon at least in principle by all forms of Buddhism. Because gender is conditioned and relative, the interdependent result of certain causes and conditions, and does not color the enlightened or the natural state of mind in any way, it should not cause us too much concern. The problem is that most people become very attached to their version of relative truth. The tendency to absolutize the relative is quite tempting, and religious people are not at all immune to this temptation. Male dominance, which is in the realm of the relative, not the realm of the absolute, has been virtually absolutized in the religious institutions of all forms of Buddhism. Thus the gender identity that is slapped on one at birth becomes the single factor that rules one's life completely, and it is assumed that the prison of gender roles that goes with a gender identity is accurate for everyone and will bring everyone a fulfilling and useful life. The problem is that for many people, neither the identity nor the role fits.

Gender roles are extremely rigid and inflexible in most societies. Not only are they rigid and inflexible but they exaggerate the minimal differences between women and men. This exaggeration is one of the most oppressive features of the prison of gender roles. For most human interactions, it is not necessary to know the sex or gender of the person with whom we are interacting, but extremes of clothing and hairstyle make it impossible to forget the gendered self of most of those people. Think how initially puzzling, but also refreshing, it is to encounter people whose gender we cannot immediately pin down. Think about the message potentially communicated by the identical dress and hairstyle of Buddhist monastics; despite artificial institutional differences imposed on Buddhist monks and nuns, they live the same lifestyle of renunciation and celibacy. Think how freeing it would be not to have to continuously negotiate gendered interactions with every person we meet. Think of the fact that if gender were absolutely fixed, as many people think it is, it would be impossible to change apparent women into apparent men and vice versa through hormones, cross-dressing, or surgery. Many societies throughout history have realized that assigned genders and gender roles do not fit everyone.

The problem with Buddhism as constituted historically is that for their relative gender practices, Buddhists have, unquestioningly and unreflectively, bought into the gender stereotypes prevalent in surrounding societies instead of asking whether those gender stereotypes correspond with Buddhist ethics and general standards of decency and equity. But it is hard to square male dominance, misogyny, and patriarchy with basic Buddhist ethics such as the ethics promulgated by the Eightfold Path. It is truly mystifying to wonder why such basic questions were never asked and Buddhists instead have been content to articulate an elevated view of the ultimate irrelevance of gender but have never tried to put it into practice. It is impossible to avoid the conclusion that Buddhist practices regarding gender at the relative level are neither skillful, wise, nor compassionate, though those values are consistently encouraged on the level of everyday ethics for ordinary people living worldly lives.

THE ULTIMATE CHALLENGE: ACCOMMODATING DIFFICULT CIRCUMSTANCES AND DISAPPOINTMENT

Buddhist teachers are fond of claiming that in the long run, obstacles and disappointment are helpful on the path of forgetting the self and attaining enlightenment. This can be difficult advice to hear or appreciate. I remember resenting teachers who gave me such advice when I complained about my many frustrations and unpleasant life circumstances. The conventional perspective is that decent people who play by the rules deserve certain things; when those things are not forthcoming, people can feel cheated. Such circumstances easily launch people into full-fledged immersion into the emotionalism of the three poisons of Buddhist analysis—aversion or aggression; grasping or desire and clinging; and ignorance. These teachings are very old in Buddhism, going back perhaps to the historical Buddha. They are also found at the very center of the famous Tibetan wheel-of-life diagram. According to Buddhism, probably to the Buddha himself, these three, being at the center of the wheel of life, are so unsatisfying as to inevitably produce a life of suffering and frustration. These emotions, which are tempting when we don't get what we want or feel we deserve, do provide temporary emotional release.

But they are unpleasant in the long run and do not work to provide the long-term relief we seek.

Especially when we don't get what we want or think we deserve, it is tempting to find someone or something to blame and to vent our rage on that person or set of circumstances. But does that really solve the problem or make things better? The poison of aggression or aversion is considered to be so corrosive that it is the fundamental Buddhist image for being in Hell. One of my foremost contributions as a Buddhist feminist theologian has been a commentary on the unworkability of "feminist rage."[2] For me, the melting of my feminist rage was one of the most surprising and unexpected results of Buddhist practice, but it was also one of the most helpful. Characteristic of my work from its beginnings, this work has not always been appreciated by other Buddhist women or by my Christian colleagues in feminist theology, who often argue that without anger or rage nothing would ever change positively, who maintain that there is something that can be called "self-righteous" anger or rage, or who didn't want to analyze whether their own sense of relief brought about by their rage really was effective at making things better.

As for the poison of desire or grasping—intensely wanting things to be different, wanting what one cannot currently have— it is so unpleasant that one wonders why anyone would indulge in such feelings time after time. It is a deeply embedded habitual pattern. That one's desires are legitimate and reasonable does nothing to change this reality. In my own case, my first direct experience of how much my suffering was intensified because I so desperately wanted things to be different, and the degree of relief that simple realization brought me, convinced me that Buddhism's counter-intuitive teachings actually were onto something. I never looked back after that, and the knowledge that resisting and fighting against one's circumstances only makes thing worse has become almost a mantra for me.

Regarding the third of the three poisons, ignorance, critics of Buddhist sensibilities may have more of a case. Obstacles develop patience, forbearance, gratitude, forgiveness, and above all, equanimity, values non-Buddhists may not prize so highly. Buddhists prize equanimity in the face of difficult circumstances. This equanimity can look to outsiders like passivity, but Buddhists claim that excessive concern over injustice can be detrimental to one's spiritual path. I have a feminist friend who has recently become a Buddhist. When we discuss some of the things that bother most feminists, she becomes visibly irritated. While these are things that also bother me, my mind remains steady and nonreactive. Noticing that, she says, "You have more equanimity than I do," to which I respond, "Yes, and because I have more equanimity, I suffer less." She agrees but still experiences the tightness of irritation.

To repeat an earlier point, I do feel that, historically, Buddhists have been too uncritical in accepting the gender practices of surrounding cultures without asking whether these practices are in accord with basic Buddhist standards of ethical decency. That level of ignoring does not lead to equanimity but instead to unethical oppression based on the local prison of gender roles. At the same time, eventually one has to choose between letting one's life simply be consumed by frustration with one's misfortunes and the unfair eventualities of one's life or choosing to experience some happiness and contentment nevertheless. In my own case, I have found that I had to learn to find joy, peace, and contentment despite not ever receiving a couple of important things I wanted very much, things most people would regard as reasonable and appropriate to making a complete life—a life partner who appreciated me and professional advancement based on nationally and internationally recognized achievements. The partners came, but their deaths were extremely untimely. Then I had to learn that believing in my story line that I was the victim of unfair misfortune was actually more painful than the sheer experience I might be undergoing in any specific moment. I learned that it is possible to heal from the trauma of difficult circumstances but only if one is willing to give up the identity of being an unfortunate person. Now, as I write these lines in an Indian hospital dealing with a serious illness, some of the lessons I have learned earlier have helped. Being in a foreign hospital is extremely frightening. Nevertheless, developing patience with difficult circumstances is far better than the alternatives of aggression or aversion or extreme grasping at the wish for things to be different than they are. Thus, I have come to believe that being a mature practitioner requires accommodating disappointment and difficult circumstances without feeling like a victim.

THREE

THE PRISON OF GENDER ROLES

When I was a girl—a preteen and an adolescent—I was miserable. Time after time, I moaned, "Why, oh why, did I have to be a girl? Girls don't get to do anything interesting or important!" I didn't have penis envy. I didn't want a boy's body. I wanted to be able to use my mind, to study and explore the world. I was smart. I loved school more than anything else, and I wanted to be able to penetrate the world that school was revealing to me, a culturally deprived farm girl in northern Wisconsin in the 1950s, a girl whose parents had not gone to high school, who barely made it economically on a marginal dairy farm and who didn't think education was important. My mother, especially, only cared that I would marry a farmer, whereupon we would take on the family farm and live a hundred feet from her for the rest of her life. She hated it that I liked school so much. I didn't want a boy's body, but from what I could tell, in that time and place, having a girl's body meant doom for my dreams to use my mind to study and explore the world. Girls grew up to dust lamps, cook, clean, and take care of men and children. Period. That was it. Sometimes I thought it was excessively cruel for a girl to be born with a high IQ and a longing to use her mind, given the limited options actually available to her.

Somehow, one day, insight dawned. I don't remember exactly how old I was, but I was still in high school, or perhaps it was even earlier in my life. I know it was well before the dawn of second-wave feminism. I have a visceral memory of being outside among milk cans in our yard. That would place the event quite early in my life, because we started shipping milk from a different location on the farm while I was still in my early teens. I was bemoaning my fate attendant on having a girl's body when suddenly I came to a physical standstill, overwhelmed by dawning insight. "There's nothing wrong with being a girl," I declared to myself. "It's the system! It's the system!"

Somehow, that insight never left, though maintaining it through the 1960s and 1970s took enormous energy and discipline. For many years thereafter, until Buddhist practice tamed it, I was plagued by my rage over what is routinely done to girls and women around the world. That rage was painful, just as my misery about being a girl had been. But until I found other resources, through Buddhist practice, with which to put my anger to better uses, rage at the system was certainly more accurate than rage directed at my own body for being a girl's body in a world that was full of obstacles to girls whose desire was to use their minds, because girls were expected to be fully available to service men and children.

What is "the system"? Let me tell you a few stories. In 1965, I was clearly at the top of my college class and was interviewing for a Woodrow Wilson Fellowship, designed to help promising students eventually become college professors. A well-meaning professor who had previously mentored me took me aside one day to shield me from the inevitable blow. "You have to realize," he said, "that you won't get a Woodrow Wilson Fellowship. You're an attractive woman. You'll get married and it will go to waste. You just can't expect them to give you such a valuable fellowship."

Now, I am average-looking, not unusually attractive, and I have never been besieged by men longing to date me or propose marriage to me. Nevertheless, on more than one occasion, I have suddenly found myself evaluated as "attractive" by a man who wasn't in a position to date me but who wanted to justify my being excluded from a privilege usually accorded to men. (I did receive the Woodrow Wilson Fellowship.) This professor was obviously comfortable with a system that would award fellowships to less deserving men over more deserving women on the basis of behaviors dictated by the prison of gender roles. Even more galling and relevant: no man has ever been denied a fellowship because in the future he might get married. Women alone are forced to bear the burdens, the downside, of marriage and reproduction, while for men, future marriage and reproduction made them more worthy, not less worthy, of fellowships.

Thus it has been for centuries as parents struggle to educate a son with indifferent academic abilities while sending their bright daughters to do menial work to earn money to educate that son. Why give sons such preference? Presumably, both the daughter and the son will marry and have children. The children of each carry forward equal amounts of genetic heritage from the parents. The daughter's children will carry a quarter of the genetic heritage of her parents, as will her brother's children. Logically and biologically, they should be equal. So why prefer the son so much? The son will have a wife to take care of his children, while the daughter will *be* the wife, taking care of children that belong to some other patrilineage and thus unable to contribute much to her natal family, at least in many family systems. And so it continues around the globe. One only has to listen to the evening news to learn that girls are physically attacked, kidnapped, and sold into marriage-slavery to keep them from becoming educated and force them into a life with no options other than servicing men and children. The tragedy is that such things seem normal in so much of the world and that people do not question why parents prefer sons to daughters, why people fight so hard to deprive women of education and agency, or why women control so few resources but are forced to do so much of the tedious, repetitive, boring work, including childcare, that is required to keep society functioning.

One more story. Early on in my life as a Buddhist scholar-practitioner, I had already located the key issue for Buddhist women—the male near-monopoly on the teacher role. Because the teacher role is by far the most important role in Buddhism, until about half the Buddhist teachers are women, Buddhism will be seriously flawed regarding gender equality and equity. So in those early years of my life as a Buddhist, I asked one of my teachers why all the teachers were men. (Although this has changed somewhat, when I asked that question in 1980, most of the teachers were men, even among Western Buddhists.) He looked shocked, and hastily replied, "Somebody has to take care of the kids!" At the time, I didn't have the wherewithal to retort properly: "Why don't you and other fathers do your fair share of taking care of the children, so that women have the time it takes to prepare to become teachers?" He then added a much more appropriate comment: "Because you haven't become a teacher yet!" That eventuality would depend on someone being willing to acknowledge me as a Buddhist teacher, however—an eventuality that finally did happen when my current Tibetan teacher, who is a woman, included me as one of her six Western teachers. I do not know whether a male Buddhist teacher would ever have been willing to acknowledge an outspoken feminist as a teacher.

EXPLORING THE PRISON OF GENDER ROLES

Later, when I became more adept at abstract thinking, I came up with a name for the pain I had experienced as a girl who wanted more than anything else to use her mind but had already internalized messages that discouraged her from believing she would be allowed to do so. I came to call it "the prison of gender roles." During that process, I also came to the startlingly simple conclusion that "women are human beings"—full human beings, not incomplete human beings lacking an essential body part. That conclusion is so simple and so compelling that it is difficult to imagine how so many things necessary to a fulfilled human life, such as being educated, having one's own spiritual life, or having pursuits beyond one's reproductive function, could be so routinely denied to women, as they still are in so many situations. Truly, under male dominance and patriarchy, whether Buddhist or Western, full humanity is denied to women. I also came to define "freedom from the prison of gender roles" as the essence of feminism, though that label is unimportant compared with getting free of that prison. As "feminism" has become a derogatory term, almost a swear word, I use it less and less.

As a Buddhist critical and constructive thinker, I find it important to thoroughly explore to what extent Buddhist thought and institutions may be caught up in promoting rather than demolishing the prison of gender roles. Sex segregation is the norm in traditional Buddhist institutions, especially monastic institutions, and nuns are frequently less well supported, both economically and in terms of the educations they receive, than are monks. According to monastic rules, every nun is subordinate to even the most recently ordained monk and must occupy an inferior position in all monastic gatherings. In their core, Buddhist teachings do not support such institutionalized sexism, but it prevails, nevertheless. These two facts about Buddhism—that its teachings are gender neutral and gender free but its institutions have been extremely male dominated—so blatantly obvious if one looks deeply and honestly, have led me to a conclusion about gender and Buddhism that I have repeated many times. Classical Buddhism presents an *intolerable contradiction between its gender-neutral and gender-egalitarian teachings and its male-dominant institutions.* But view and practice should support each other, not undermine each other!

Because its teachings are so genuinely gender neutral and gender free, Buddhism may involve a deeper conflict between its views and its practices regarding gender than other major religions. In that conflict, clearly, views should trump institutional practices. That they do not indicates how strong a hold the prison of gender roles has on Buddhist intellects. That explains the embarrassed reactions of teachers who are challenged to defend problematic Buddhist practices and then recite the slogan that enlightened mind is beyond gender, so, therefore, there can be no problems regarding gender in Buddhism. But that comment is quite far off the mark. Instead, the same disciplines we apply to deconstructing the presumption of self that relies on skandhas, ayatanas, dhatus, and all the other Buddhist methods that have been used to deconstruct the egos that feel so real to us, should be applied to the ego composed of gender roles and gender norms, which, if anything, feels *even more real.* To repeat the words of Zen master Dogen: "To study the way of enlightenment is to study the self. To study the self is to forget the self." We could say that all of Buddhist practice is about "forgetting the self" that we have believed in for so long and that causes us so much suffering. Generally, we do understand that the only way to forget the self is to first study it thoroughly. Why do we shy away when it comes to studying the gendered self?

Thus, in demonstrating how clinging to gender identity subverts enlightenment, we must first thoroughly look into the prison of gender roles before we take pride in the Buddhist teachings and practice that could subdue the prison of gender roles if we actually applied them. Otherwise, as one of my friends put it, we are left with a Buddhism that has a great deal of potential for deconstructing gender, but little has come of that potential. What is revealed by such a gaze is not especially pleasant. It is difficult to take in all the androcentrism, male dominance, and misogyny that have kept both women and men trapped in the prison of gender roles. This deep gaze includes exploring all the ways that women are complicit in maintaining the prison of gender roles, by willingly making themselves into sex objects, among other things. Men often become frustrated with feminist language because they feel they are being blamed for things they didn't set up and don't control, and there is validity to that claim. Although, by and large, men gain more from the prison of gender roles than do women (which is why men are often reluctant to give those roles up), women and men together construct that prison. It is unlikely that one sex will demolish it single-handedly.

The problem with conventional approaches to gender is that the immediate, often unavoidable perception that someone is either a man or a woman instantaneously brings with it a whole host of assumptions, expectations, and restrictions. There is no problem with the immediate perception. Gender designations as conventional, agreed-upon labels are harmless and somewhat useful, just as words and labels, by themselves, are not a problem but are necessary for everyday communication. It would be hard to deny that most human beings are either males or females. That mere designation is not what launches the prison of gender roles. The problem lies with all the baggage that is imposed on the perception by long-standing training in conventional gender stereotypes.

For example, thinking about my own experience, I know that I have a female body, and in my full-figured case, that is quite obvious to others as well. But that really doesn't give people much reliable information about me, and it gives them no information that associates me with the stereotypical female gender role. It does not mean that I must bear children, or even that I can. It certainly doesn't mean that I like or adore children. It does not mean that I necessarily have a gentle, nonaggressive demeanor as opposed to a violent or nasty temperament. It does not even guarantee my primary sexual orientation, which has been guessed wrong almost as often as it has been guessed right by observers, both women and men. My female sex is not a reliable guide to my interests and concerns. I care little for many of the things that are supposed to interest women, but I also am interested in some things that are generally thought to be of more interest to women than to men. In short, though my sex may be the first fact about me that registers, it tells people almost nothing about me. It is especially irrelevant to making people aware of things about myself that are important to me. Nevertheless, though my female body doesn't translate into anything essential about me, a great deal has been projected onto it by society, by religions, and by individuals who think that the shape of my body reveals something about me that is intrinsically existing, something on which it is valid to pin all sorts of meanings and limitations. That is how the mere perception turns into the clinging that imprisons. That is the *prison* of gender roles, as opposed to *mere noting* of someone's sex.

Questioning the relationship between a phenomenon and the meanings we pin onto it is a familiar Buddhist discipline. Its most familiar form is the basic instruction to not be so ideologically fixated on our thoughts but simply to let them pass through our consciousness, noting them without attaching to them. My own way of phrasing this instruction to students is this: "Just because you have a thought doesn't mean you need to believe in it." This discipline should be ongoing, on and off the cushion. In fact, forgetting to apply that instruction off the cushion is responsible for a good deal of our misery.

To begin to break down the prison of gender roles, we have to rigorously apply this discipline to our knee-jerk reactions, our thoughts about someone, based on any aspect of their appearance—sex, race, color, culture, age, seemingly feminized or masculinized affectations—whatever we may encounter. Even applying this discipline to merely noting people's sex without projecting so much onto our perception is difficult, largely because it has not been included in our repertoire of Buddhist practices. It is instructive to encounter situations in which we have to interact with people without being certain about their sex—as in the example of the yellow-swaddled infants discussed earlier. It would be enlightening to be able to encounter such situations more frequently. For adults, written communication with people whose names do not immediately reveal their sex to someone unfamiliar with the gendering of names in a different culture can be revealing. In some cultures, both men and women can have the same name. Why do we think we need to know someone's sex to be able to interact with them?

If, by whatever means necessary and possible, we discipline ourselves to break the link between our perception of someone's sex and a whole host of expectations about them, we at least begin to make some inroads into the prison of gender roles. We would no longer say, "She's a girl. She's going to be a mother, not a STEM professional." "That's a boy. He should be playing with trucks, not dolls. He has to be made tough and aggressive. He should play football, not the violin." Much more important, at least for Buddhists, we would no longer assume that women won't be dharma teachers or, if they do become teachers, prohibit them from teaching men, as is done in some monastic situations. In the Tibetan situation, people could no longer look at a baby girl and conclude, "She's a girl. She can't be the rebirth of the teacher we're looking for." The current Dalai Lama has said that he would be pleased if the next Dalai Lama is female.[1] But would Tibetan Buddhists, whose practices are quite male dominant, be able to recognize their leader is such a form? Or would the link between perception and projection (girl, therefore not Dalai Lama) be so strong that the prison of gender roles would survive unscathed, despite clear teachings that enlightened mind is beyond gender, neither male nor female?

CONVENTIONAL BUDDHIST PERSPECTIVES ON GENDER ROLES

The prison of gender roles imprisons all, both women and men. But, under the contingent, humanly created, and interdependently arisen social arrangements in place from before the beginnings of Buddhism to almost the present day, it affects women and men quite differently. Part of the way it has affected men and women differently is by giving men the freedom and leisure to do time-consuming Buddhist practices and write Buddhist texts. By contrast, according to many of the texts these men wrote, one of the five woes attendant on the unfortunate rebirth of having a female body is that women are constrained to spend all their time taking care of men and children.[2] These rules, so convenient for men, freed them to study and write Buddhist texts while women were kept too busy to study and write such texts themselves. Given that men and women have rather different experiences of the conventional world bound by the prison of gender roles, women might have written quite different texts, had they had such opportunities![3] The prison of gender roles hems women in far more than it inhibits men. In fact, it weighs so lightly on men that they often feel that gender does not apply to them at all but only to women. Men are just normal human beings unencumbered by gender—or so men claim, because that is how it feels to them. So often they feel that they don't have to cut through the prison of gender roles. It is my impression that this hubris on the part of men makes it easy for them not to recognize the difference between their conventional egos, bound up with filling the male gender role in a male-dominated society, and enlightened mind beyond gender, neither male nor female. Thus, they might easily have done a thoroughgoing analysis of ego in terms of the categories available to them, even gaining some insight into enlightened mind beyond gender, without thorough analysis of the gendered ego residing in the prison of gender roles. Some liberation and realization would be attendant on that insight. But we must also remember the Buddhist principle that no one is truly and completely free so long as some are not free. Fully articulating the limits binding the gendered ego probably requires input from those who experience the prison of gender roles more intimately and oppressively.

Buddhism's views about gender throughout its long history are easily summarized. On the one hand, the more normative view is that gender is ultimately irrelevant because enlightened mind is neither male nor female but beyond gender. However, that view had little impact on Buddhist institutions or everyday life. The more popular and pervasive view is that gender matters a great deal and it is far more fortunate to be a man than a woman. In fact, traditional Buddhists commonly believed that a woman could not become enlightened in her female body but had to be reborn as a man first. Thus, women were given practices and prayers to help them secure a male rebirth in their next lives.

When I give talks on Buddhism and gender, I often tell a story about the time I gave my first talk on "Buddhism and feminism" at an international conference on Buddhist-Christian dialogue at the University of Hawaii. The Japanese Buddhist male delegates to the conference didn't talk to me, but they talked to my male Western colleagues, who reported their comments to me, which were along these lines: "What's the matter with that crazy American woman, thinking feminism is relevant to Buddhism? We can understand Christian women having a problem. After all, all the priests are men and Jesus was a man. But we Buddhists solved all those problems long ago. Deserving women are reborn as men!"

Western women are often infuriated (as I was) when we first hear that Buddhism routinely taught that female rebirth is the result of negative karma, as it's often put. But the whole thing is much more subtle. For one thing, those teachings are often imprecisely stated. Most precisely put, according to traditional Buddhist teachings, female rebirth is *unfortunate*, not *inferior*. It is crucial to state Buddhist teachings on this point precisely—unfortunate is not the same thing as inferior. We Western women were also socialized in male-dominant cultural contexts, but we were clearly taught from early on that we are inferior to men. Inferiority means being made of inferior materials, and in traditional Western sources, there is no subtlety on that point.[4] Unfortunate, by contrast, simply means that one encounters difficult circumstances that are accidental to one's experience, not inherent and inevitable in one's being.

In Buddhist teachings, if female birth is inferior, it is inferior because it involves so much misfortune and woe. This is not an unreasonable conclusion in situations in which girls were denied education because they would not be able to use it. They would be married off at puberty or earlier, and their lives would be completely devoted to childbearing, child-rearing, and domestic and agricultural labor. Many of their children would die and many of them would die in childbirth. Many women would have to deal with co-wives. Who would want such a life if there was any other option! Yet it describes the life that a large portion of the world's women still have to endure and that the vast majority of women endured until recently. For Buddhists, such a situation is truly unfortunate and woe-filled because people who have to endure such conditions are much less likely to encounter that enlightened state of mind beyond gender, neither male nor female, to which Buddhist teachers love to refer. That is the dharmic reason why breaking down the prison of gender roles should be of such urgency for Buddhists.

Buddhist traditions include much more detailed teachings on what makes a woman's life less than fortunate. First of all, it was taken for granted that women would have to endure "the three subserviences." This is not a uniquely Buddhist idea but was taken over from the Indian culture of the day. It also prevailed in the East Asian cultures into which Buddhism later migrated. According to this code, a woman should never be independent and in charge of her own life. In youth, her father should control her; in the prime of life, her husband; and in old age, her son. In fact, the only independent women were prostitutes, who play a significant role in many Buddhist stories. This dictum that women must always be under the control of men is probably behind the infamous "eight heavy rules" that subordinate the senior nun to even the most junior monk. The Buddha is said to have imposed these rules on nuns as the price of their ordination into the monastic sangha, though many doubt the authenticity of that story.

Another list is that of the "five stations a woman cannot attain"— having been the Hindu gods Brahma and Indra, having been a great king, having been an emperor, and having been an irreversible bodhisattva.[5] The purpose of this list is to explain why Buddhas are never women, rather than to limit women in their present lives. It was believed that in order to become a Buddha, one had first to have held all the samsaric stations on this list, none of which were possible for a female to attain. It would still be logically possible for there to be a female Buddha, however; a being could have held all those stations as a man and then been reborn as a woman who would become a Buddha in that life. That possibility does not seem to have been explored, probably because historically most Buddhists have believed that a male who led an upright, meritorious life would never again be reborn as a female.

The third list, "the five woes," is the most important. The "five woes" are menstruation, pregnancy, childbirth, having to leave one's natal family to live with one's husband's family, and having to spend all one's energy taking care of one's husband and children. Three of these are biological and two social, which means that different methods would be required to ameliorate them. The social woes are obviously due to social institutions humans have set up and could change. The biological woes represent a male evaluation of female biology—an evaluation that women might not share, especially when they can control their fertility.

What has always impressed me about this list is that traditional Buddhists *admit* that women's lives under male dominance are "woeful," deeply problematic, and unsatisfactory, something no other male-dominated religion concedes. In other cases, women's lives under male dominance are romanticized and glorified, but Buddhists are more realistic. Traditional Buddhists agree with feminist claims about male dominance—it's unpleasant for women!

Valuing compassion, Buddhists had to find ways to ease the suffering of beings currently born as women. A modern person would say, "Change the social institutions." In fact, that is essentially what feminists are saying. But, apparently, it seemed more possible under premodern conditions to change women into men than to change social institutions so they would not be male dominant. (Sex change is a frequent motif in Buddhist stories.) Buddhists may not have been wrong about changing social institutions so that they were less male dominant before the advent of modern medicine and reliable, widely available birth control. That is why it was so revolutionary and so crucial that Buddhist women had the option of choosing a nonreproductive lifestyle as a nun. That is one of the reasons why it is so important that nuns' ordination again becomes available in all Buddhist lineages.

Do Buddhist *women* agree with these traditional assessments about being female? Upon learning that I am a feminist, some Western women have said to me, pertly and with an air of superiority, "But I *like* being a woman!" Perhaps, similarly, more traditional Buddhist women don't mind their situations. Are Western feminists making objections for them that they do not share? Apart from the *Therigatha* ("The Songs of the Female Elders"), few Buddhist texts were composed by women, even though there are many portraits of women in those texts. However, recent scholarship gives us information previously unavailable to Western Buddhists. One such work is the autobiography of a Buddhist nun, Orgyan Chokyi, from the late seventeenth and early eighteenth centuries, who lived in the mountains of what is present-day Nepal.[6] There is much to say about her story, though here I will focus on her comments on being born female.[7] Because some contemporary Asian Buddhists and Western social scientists claim that complaints about women's lives under male dominance must be influenced by Western feminism, Orgyan Chokyi's assessments of being born as a female are highly relevant, given that they predate Western feminism by centuries. A typical comment combines disenchantment with both the female body and male sexual desire:

When I ponder our female bodies
I am sorrowful; impermanence rings clear.

When men and women couple—creating more life—
Happiness is rare, but suffering is felt for a long time.

May I not be born again in a female body.
May the mare not be born as a mare.

The steed follows yet another mare.
When I see the shamelessness of men,
[I think:] May I be born in a body that will sustain the precepts.[8]

Another helpful study, published in 2004, is based on years of
fieldwork in contemporary Ladakh.[9] After detailing the difficulties nuns face in trying to maintain themselves in this sparsely
populated region of India, the author summarizes local attitudes,
male and female, monastic and lay, about birth as a female. "The
bottom line is clear. No Buddhist in her right mind desires a female body."[10] Reading such reports is difficult and saddening. But
it is important to be clear-eyed and unromantic about Buddhist
women's lives and their attitudes about female birth under traditional conditions before we claim that "feminism" is irrelevant
to Buddhists, whether Asian or Western. Whether a woman or a
man, who would want to live under such conditions?

Alongside these widespread opinions and reports about the
woes of female birth are other equally authoritative and important comments. There is a well-established tradition of Buddhist
protest of the conditions and understandings that led to the evaluation that women's lives are woeful. From the beginnings of
Buddhism throughout its entire history, there is another stream
of claims—claims that those who denigrate women and insist
that human beings cannot become enlightened as women are
mistaken. Stories were told that elevated the status of women
who were barely mentioned in earlier versions of those same
stories. This other tradition, which I have begun to call "indig-

enous Buddhist feminism," never displaced the more dominant tradition that evaluated female birth as woeful, in part because Buddhist institutions supported the male-dominant traditions much more adequately. These traditions and texts are important because they effectively counter claims that "feminism" is foreign, non-Buddhist, and unnecessary for Buddhists.

However, this other tradition is also much less well known to Western Buddhists. The androcentric model of humanity firmly entrenched in the minds of many Western scholars, to be discussed in chapter 5, meant that those scholars could not see a great deal of material that did not conform to their own androcentrism. Many generalizations that are well established in Western understandings of Buddhism will be modified as these materials, beginning with the *Therigatha*, become better known to Western Buddhists.

GENDER ROLES IN COMPARATIVE PERSPECTIVE

The prison of gender roles has always been justified as being based on biological constraints. But how much are gender roles constrained by the fact that men inseminate and women give birth? Do these facts necessarily mean that women must take care of men and children in a way that is not required of men, while men are free to spend their time writing books, preparing to become Buddhist teachers, and using their minds doing other interesting and important things? The presumption that women should bear unequal and much heavier obligations for childcare and routine domestic labor is the source both of my own youthful despair over having a girl's body and of Buddhist comments on why it is more fortunate to be a man than a woman. Indeed, unequal parenting responsibilities between males and females seems endemic to mammalian species, to the point that one wonders how anyone could posit "intelligent design." At least regarding equal parenting, avian species seem to be far more evolved than mammals! And shared parenting responsibilities would seem to be more equitable for both men and women as well as psychologically healthier for children.

Can we learn anything useful about best practices regarding sex and gender for human beings in general or for Buddhists from comparative studies of nonhuman animal behavior, on the one hand, and from studying human societies around the world, on the other hand? Regarding the behavior of nonhuman animals, especially regarding other mammals, preliminary impressions include stark warnings. Males are predisposed to spend enormous amounts of energy fighting with other males, mainly for sexual access to females and secondarily for territory. As a result, only a few males mate. One wonders what the rest of the males do with their lives, or why females and males are born in relatively equal numbers? In domesticated species, what happens to the extra males is clear. Few of them will mate. To tame their aggression, most of them will be castrated so that they can be made useful to human beings, a fate especially common for horses and cattle. My three beloved male cats could not possibly live together indoors with me if they had not been castrated. Otherwise, they would be constantly fighting with each other, to say nothing of marking their territory with their foul-smelling spray. (To be clear, this is not about whether males or females are superior. Female cats can also have great difficulty sharing small territories.) In other cases, most males will be butchered for human food. On the farm where I grew up, half the calves that were born to keep the cows producing milk were males. Without exception, at eight weeks old they were sold as veal calves. Other than that, they were useless. Even on a small marginal farm in the 1950s, we did not keep a bull because they are expensive and dangerous. An artificial insemination service was much more practical. Some years ago, I participated in a small faculty seminar tasked to reflect on gender roles in an imaginative, wide-ranging manner. Noting that millions of cows but only a few hundred bulls live in Wisconsin, the dairy state, one of the men concluded that males need to take stock of their behavior and of what they contribute to society. Only a few males are needed to keep a species going!

Any relevance of these observations about cattle for human society may seem far-fetched—until one considers how much of their time and energy human males spend fighting for territory with other human males, and how much human females are now also drawn into such fighting, as it depends less on upper-body strength and more on brain power. Sexual predation is often connected with such fighting. Raping or enslaving women whose male family members have been killed fighting with other men is going on as I write these words. It is not a thing of the past. Is such behavior in any way elevated above the nonhuman animal behavior we see depicted every day on beautifully filmed nature shows? Buddhist thinking about realms of existence always posits significant distinctions between the animal realm and the human realm. Animals are said to lack the ability to explore new ways of doing things, whereas humans are supposed to be characterized by our ability to discriminate, weigh options, and make better choices. But one has to wonder! Are human choices to constantly be at war with one another biologically imperative? Do men really have no choice but to fight with each other nonstop, as do male animals? Is sexual predation, or at least constant interest in sex, hardwired into male bodies? At least for some women contemplating these questions, it is hard to imagine how human beings could regard such states of mind as normal or desirable. Do men find them equally unpalatable? In some cases, they must, but perhaps not in large enough numbers yet to put a stop to such habitual behaviors.

For Buddhists, however, such habitual patterns can never be excused simply as due to "hardwiring," biological fiat, or habits so deeply engrained that they cannot be overcome. We are asked to overcome habitual tendencies that are even more deeply engrained than propensities to fight or seduce, at least according to Buddhist teachings, which also proclaim that we have the ability and the disciplines to do so. As Buddhists, we are consistently asked to deconstruct our conventional egos, that sense of being a separate, permanent entity that feels so real to us and easily causes us to conflict with other people or to desire them sexually and emotionally. Successfully deconstructing that ego would certainly have a direct impact on our aggressive or lustful tendencies.

Clearly, sexual restraint is considered to be possible for both women and men. It is a well-known part of Buddhist disciplines. However, violence and militarism seem to be much deeper problems. Majority Buddhist societies have never succeeded in doing without armies and warfare, despite clear Buddhist preferences for nonharming. Twentieth- and twenty-first-century societies with either large Buddhist or majority Buddhist populations have engaged in a number of highly criticized military operations, though these examples can be countered with the well-known example of the Dalai Lama and his advocacy of nonviolence. What has gone awry with Buddhist projects to deconstruct ego, if even Buddhist societies are still so prone to military solutions to social problems? Perhaps the links between gender and ego have not been explored thoroughly enough. Perhaps deconstructing ego by teaching about skandhas, ayatanas, and dhatus is too abstract to take effect, whereas it would be more effective to teach directly about tendencies to which men and women caught in the prison of gender roles are still prone. Perhaps men need to hear more directly about how to address tendencies such as feeling that their dignity depends on being tough and aggressive or having multiple consorts, and women need to hear that having a man in their lives will not necessarily make them happy. Those gender-based dimensions of ego certainly do keep samsara going and certainly do subvert enlightenment.

To return to the most pervasive and most destructive part of the prison of gender roles, the requirement that women do most of the child-rearing, the question is not fundamentally an issue of biological determinism. For human beings it is not a question of whether females are the ones who give birth, but rather the question is how much their birth-giving *must* inhibit them from other activities. Despite the fact that men are often desperate for male offspring, no one expects men to find complete fulfillment in their role as fathers, to define themselves completely with their parenthood, or to spend all their time filling that role. How, then, could women, who are equally competent and intelligent, be expected to make a complete life of their parenthood? That such demands are sometimes made of women does not render them fairer or more reasonable. Thoughtful women often conclude that under contemporary conditions in societies whose economies are based largely on service and professional occupations, fathers' doing significant childcare, even for young children, is the missing ingredient in making women's lives bearable. It would also be a missing ingredient in humanizing men who are otherwise much too identified with a stress-filled, competitive, aggressive version of a male gender role.

Unfortunately, such developments are inhibited by romantic stereotypes about male and female gender roles, which are largely based on outdated ideals, most of which were never practical for large numbers of people. Much contemporary Western folklore about gender roles is based on a fantasy of an ideal time in the past when men provided for women and children while passive, economically dependent females waited for males to "bring home the bacon." But this impractical ideal of women being economically incompetent and dependent on men has never been how most people have lived or could live. First of all, only in economies in which home and workplace are widely separated and everyone is dependent on money, on wage labor, could such a division of labor between men and women even occur. It was largely a goal for upper classes during the industrial age and in some other societies. Being able to afford to keep women idle was a sign of power and prestige, but such practices were never practical for middle- and working-class people, even during industrialization. In the foraging, horticultural, and agricultural economies that sustained humanity for most of its history before industrial and service economies became dominant, humans would have starved to death if they had tried to survive on men's economic activity alone. Women simply have not abdicated economic roles to find fulfillment in motherhood alone in most societies throughout most of history. Thus the statistics, alarming to some, showing more women and more mothers being employed for wage labor outside their homes only represent a return to a situation that is far more usual than women having no economic role and being expected to devote their entire lives to motherhood.

Nor have women traditionally reared their children alone, isolated behind four walls, as this fantasy is completed in many people's imaginations. Nuclear families that isolate one woman inside a house with her children while her husband "brings home the bacon" are a recent norm. Most people throughout history have had help with child-rearing from relatives and community networks. Yet, when Hillary Clinton wrote a book titled *It Takes a Village* (1996), she was pilloried by conservatives who wanted to keep women isolated behind those walls, tied down with their own children, alone, even though there have always been other options.

This fantasy keeps the prison of gender roles alive and well, whether or not it is successful or corresponds to any reality. A large part of this fantasy-prison is the claim that only men should fill certain occupations, mainly ones that are well paid and prestigious, which is the only way that the role of "bringing home the bacon" could possibly be confined to men. (When Sandra Day O'Connor, the first female justice on the U.S. Supreme Court, tried to find employment as an attorney after graduating from Stanford Law School, forty law firms declined to interview her because they didn't hire female attorneys. She found employment only after she offered to work as a deputy county attorney for no salary.)[11] If only men are suited for these occupations, then there needs to be some inherent link between having a penis and the job requirements. But what does a penis, and only a penis, do? It spurts semen, but, based on all the TV ads for erectile dysfunction drugs, it doesn't even seem to do that all that reliably. What does having a penis have to do with being a successful lawyer? Having a penis tends to correlate with greater upper body strength, which is a relevant criterion for some occupations, such as some kinds of agriculture, logging, heavy industry, or playing American football. But our society does not run on those occupations. It runs on occupations that require brain power, not upper body strength, and nothing suggests any correlation between having a penis and having greater brain power.

Because nothing about male biology makes men better lawyers, doctors, and so forth than women, the only recourse left to preserve the prison of gender roles is to insist that, rather than having men share childcare, women be left with the majority of that job. Men don't want to limit their careers by doing part-time childcare during the years it is required, but for women, such a loss is not considered to be a problem or taken seriously. One justification for the fact that women earn less than men for the same work is that they have taken more time off work than men to take care of family members, thereby losing seniority!

Granted, individuals and couples receive almost no help from society in general or from employers in negotiating ways that both women and men could keep their careers on track while also caring for their families or (for employees who are less career-oriented and more concerned about simply making ends meet) negotiating ways that both women and men could do so with more ease and less stress. Remember that early in second-wave feminism, we dreamed of job-sharing and shorter work weeks, so that everyone who wanted to do so could experience not only meaningful work, one of the great needs for a satisfying human life, but also more time to do other things, such as playing with children and creating culture. But then, we envisioned dismantling the prison of gender roles. We have a long way to go!

MEN AND THE PRISON OF GENDER ROLES

When women talk about the prison of gender roles or about sexism and patriarchy, it can sound as if they affect only women, leaving men unscathed. There is much less awareness of the downside of the prison of gender roles for men and also much less willingness to acknowledge that there is a downside for men. But, to dismantle that prison, it is critically important to look at it from both sides. I have frequently alluded to my pain over being a girl who wanted to use my mind to explore the world but was being forced into the female gender role of caring for men and children. But had I been a boy, I would have faced extreme pressure to stay on that farm and continue barely being able to make a living while working extremely hard. Though my mother castigated me severely for ruining her life by not planning to stay in Rhinelander when I grew up, at least I wasn't a boy, who would have had no reason at all, in her eyes, not to inherit the farm and the lifestyle she so desperately wanted to pass on. Conveniently, that farmer boy she wanted me to marry never showed up.

When I taught courses in gender studies at the university, I would often ask for students' impression of the pluses and minuses of both male and female gender roles. Most of the students in these courses were women, and they were adept at pointing out disadvantages of the female gender role and advantages of the male role. As for the advantages of being female or the female gender role, many of them stated they were glad they were the ones who were going to get to be pregnant and have the babies. (Compare this to the Buddhist male evaluations of pregnancy and childbirth discussed above.) But when it came to disadvantages of the male gender role, they simply drew a blank. Nothing.

"What about military service?" I would prod, citing what men of my Vietnam-era generation would bitterly say when pressed into discussions of male and female comparative advantages and disadvantages. That didn't seem to register, even though men throughout history have borne a disproportionate share of the miseries of being at war. This may be the case, even when we factor in all the costs borne by women who have been raped by enemy soldiers; lost husbands, sons, brothers, and fathers in warfare; been killed themselves as "collateral damage"; or had their homes and livelihoods destroyed. By the time I was teaching gender studies, the United States had an all-volunteer army and increasing numbers of women who sought upward mobility through military service, which probably made the specter of forced military service remote to my students.

The best response to that question I ever received came, unsought, from the great Buddhist poet Allen Ginsberg. I was once asked to give a reading from *Buddhism after Patriarchy* at a Buddhist meditation center. At the end of my reading, Allen Ginsberg was standing beside me, listening attentively. In the conversation that followed, he said simply, "The problem with being a man is that you're expected to have it up all the time." Obviously, he wasn't talking about penises. He was talking about a cultural attitude that men should always be "on the make," sexually, economically, culturally, and in every other way. What do advertisements say about men? They should be dominant, period, never flaccid in any way about any endeavor or enterprise. They should be omni-competent, never at a loss regarding anything. Obviously, most men cannot meet that standard, any more than women can ever be attractive enough, pliant and nonthreatening enough, or nurturing enough to satisfy the demands of the female gender role, especially as men envision it. The male gender role may literally be killing men, whose stressful lifestyles give them a shorter lifespan than women under modern conditions. That was not the norm until relatively recently.

But do men take the prison of gender roles seriously? Do they question the pressure and need to dominate at least *somebody*, to be able to feel that "at least I'm better than _____?" The quest for higher status in a hierarchy seems to be strong and helps explain, among other things, why professional men, especially in academia, are so threatened by and so jealous of women who are more successful. It may also help explain racism and other ethnic tensions between different groups of men and how easily such tensions lead to conflicts and violence.

Men may express sexual frustration sometimes, especially when those almighty penises won't perform, complaining to women, "All you have to do is lie there! I have to do all the work." Suddenly the sex they are always seeking is "work." Or they may complain that they are expected to "provide," to be *the* breadwinner, while also being too embarrassed to have their wives work for money. (Their wives have always "worked" without earning any money.) If their wives do work for money, as is now much more common, they think that women should still do all the work at home, which they define as "women's work," while they should be able to relax at home after their hard day of work away from the home! That women work the "double shift," working both at work and at home, remains the single biggest complaint of women and source of domestic tension. Of course, childcare arrangements, parent-teacher conferences, and emergencies such as children's illness or injury are all up to wives to manage. Men would be penalized at work for taking care of such concerns. Women may lose their jobs if meeting their children's needs interferes with their work, but that's minor compared to men maintaining their image as the primary breadwinners. Men could refuse to take on being the primary breadwinner in favor of more egalitarian arrangements, but they usually don't, sometimes because employers and society at large are dead set against modifying the prison of gender roles in any way.

The situation regarding the prison of gender roles has become quite strange in the Western world. Women can now do almost everything that used to be characterized as "men's work," including coming home from war in body bags. But men? They still seem intensely to fear being "feminine" or being "feminized." The humorous underbelly of their fear of femininity is their fear of skirts—for them, not when women wear them. While pants are comfortable and appropriate for many tasks, which is why women now wear them freely everywhere, so are skirts. Skirts are much cooler in hot weather, which is why indigenous dress for men in most tropical climates includes some version of a skirt. They are much more comfortable for the sitting meditation that Buddhists engage in for hours. They are part of the religious garb for men, especially for powerful religious leaders, in many religions, both Asian and Western. During the most recent papal election, the sight of so many men who routinely suppress women running around in their clerical skirts almost made me sick. In my own Buddhist community, the senior teachers need some sort of distinctive dress, but it probably would involve a monastic-style skirt, which is deeply troubling to the men involved. One of them is reported to have told our teacher, "I'll do anything for you, but please don't make me wear a skirt." I love to tease men about their fear of skirts and often have remarked about the utility of skirts in the presence of one of the male senior teachers. He responds, somewhat fiercely, "Rita, you'll never get us to give up our trousers." Once I replied,

"If you can't give up your pants, how are you ever going to give up your ego?" He conceded that I had a point.

This fear of skirts must reveal something deeper, some need to hang on to something that men *don't do* that makes them *"not-women."* When it becomes impossible or difficult to keep women out of something that used to be a male preserve—education and professional competence, for example—men still seem to hang on to something women do that they don't do, as a refuge of dignity and maleness. In my classes on religion and gender, I would often say that to finish breaking out of the prison of gender roles, men needed to become more "feminine," just as women had already become more "masculine." Even my brightest and most capable male students, who usually "got" far more of what I was teaching about gender than most of the female students, would look uncomfortable at the point, would look as if they were desperately searching for an "exit" and might become sick. This is where male dominance shades into misogyny—fear and hatred of things "feminine" and, especially, fear and hatred of *being* feminine (for a man). If that fear is not subdued, the prison of gender roles is still intact and a gendered ego holds one prisoner to samsara, no matter how clearly one gets the logic of egolessness and believes in it.

WOMEN AS SEX OBJECTS AND WOMEN'S COMPLICITY IN THAT ROLE

For many women, myself included, quite early in our life, we realized that society prefers men to women and grants them higher status. My parents did not communicate to me that they would have preferred a son to a daughter, and I truly don't think they did, though I never discussed that issue with them. Nevertheless, the message that boys are generally preferred to girls came through early, perhaps from religion more than anything else. I remember clearly reflecting during my preschool years on the fact that both God and Jesus, the most important people in the world, were men. "What does that mean about me, a girl?" I wondered. In the tiny log cabin my parents had built was a small framed picture of an angel protecting two children, a boy and a girl, who were crossing a raging torrent on a rickety bridge that looked as if it could fall down any second. The angel was radiantly beautiful and had wonderful wings. I loved her because she looked like me. "The angels are women! There's a place for me," I happily concluded.

Some years later, I was being prepared for confirmation by the local pastor. He was instructing about gender roles. For girls, that meant being married, if at all possible, and having children. Single women did do wonderful work in the church, he said, but it was so much better if they could be married. As married women, they should be obedient and serve their husbands in every way. Why? We know that men are superior to women and more important than women from the fact that both God and Jesus are men, he said. I put up my hand. "But the angels are women," I protested. "No," I was told. "Angels are also men. Artists painted them incorrectly, so that they look feminine, but they are men, too!" The incident was so painful that those memories were repressed until years later when I began to study Hindu goddesses and their relevance to Western women seeking positive imagery for themselves. A large copy of that picture from my parents' home now hangs in my bedroom, along with an aerial photograph of that farm, my PhD certificate, some of my dharma names, posters of presentations I have given, and awards I have received.

Women socialized in male-dominant societies, which today includes most women in the world, easily develop a sense of inferiority and shame early in our lives. We see that we are less valued than our brothers, even if we are smarter and more obedient. When I was a girl, it was still the case that sports were simply unavailable to girls, and physical competence was discouraged. I received an early lesson in the politics of gender roles when I bragged that I could run faster than any of the boys. I was told not to do things like that, not to be better than the boys at anything because men find competence in women unattractive, which would make things difficult for me later when I needed to date and find a husband. That proved to be an accurate prediction—another indication of how imprisoning gender roles are for both men and women! Their imprisonment in the male gender role makes it difficult for men to appreciate intelligent, highly educated, and competent women as potential life partners. When I was a girl, we were frequently told that soon we would be much more eager to have the boys like us than to excel in school or be physically active and strong. Girls like me were endlessly taunted with the claim that women didn't need a college degree, but only went to college to get their "Mrs." degree.

Is it any wonder that women often turn out to have low self-esteem, to be tentative, and to lack confidence? Although, of course, there are exceptions in both directions, anyone who has taught undergraduates extensively cannot fail to notice that female students, even when they are "better" students, in the sense that they are more disciplined and studious, often are not fond of innovative thinking, preferring established conventions to new hypotheses, and they don't engage in bold thinking themselves. One of the most difficult things for many women to do, especially younger women socialized under male dominance, is to question or resist male authority. Such resistance is especially difficult because it brings immediate reprimands from men, reprimands that reinforce feelings of inferiority. Such young women easily become more interested in pleasing men than in thinking independently, in thinking thoughts of which the men might not approve. Thus, in the Buddhist case, for example, if local male religious authorities tell local women that *bhikshuni* ordination is something they don't need or want and that it is a foreign idea that stems from Western feminism, local women usually conclude that they are not interested in full ordination. Then, both local monks and local women, often novice nuns, maintain that conviction, even though more extensive knowledge of Buddhist sources clearly demonstrates that the normative Buddhist sangha consists of four types of disciples, including fully ordained nuns, not the three kinds of disciples found in the early Pali Buddhist tradition of Theravada and Tibetan communities that no longer ordain nuns.

For many women, however, the link between early socialization to their own inferiority to men and later behaviors is the extent to which women focus on being sexually attractive to men and become complicit in being sex objects. Such behaviors are superficially different from those of women agreeing with male religious authorities about their own need to be subordinate to men, but they share a larger objective—women with low self-esteem can gain relief if they please men. Being sexually attractive and available sexually is one of the easiest ways for women to please men. That ability, however, depends on youth and beauty—as readily admitted by both women and men who use each other to get what each wants. This mutual game or dance proceeds on many levels, from provocative dress to easy sexual availability.

Something that truly puzzles me is the sexually provocative way in which women who want to be taken seriously professionally will, nevertheless, dress. Women routinely show a great deal more skin than the men with whom they work. Men playing in a symphony orchestra are covered from neck to cuffs and down to their ankles, whereas the women playing violins next to them often have their upper bodies largely exposed. The same pertains to news anchors on news shows, which now frequently have female and male coanchors. The female anchors often wear short skirts as well. Why? The men and women work in the same climate-controlled environment, so one would think that either the men must be too warm or the women too cold, given how differently they are dressed. Interestingly, in the few cases in which larger women fill such roles, they rarely display so much skin. But for men, whether they are young, slim, and in good shape or whether they are old and fat, the uniform is the same. Why do women so readily concede to being distracting for the wrong reasons? Men choose not to dress themselves as sex objects. Perhaps this is one male behavior that women could profitably adopt.

Dress codes vary considerably from culture to culture and cause a great deal of contention. I do not concede the thesis that women are responsible for men's sexually predatory behavior, no matter how they might dress. Provocative clothing is never a valid excuse for rape, and it is appalling that such an excuse sometimes works in court. Nor do I concede that men cannot control themselves sexually, which requires women to be either kept totally invisible in private realms or, if in public spaces, completely veiled and thus also invisible. How can men claim superiority but also claim that they cannot control themselves sexually unless women are either invisible or covered from head to toe? Nor do I concede the thesis of many young women that women's liberation is a matter of being able to appear practically naked in public. One sore point in early second-wave feminism was the use of women's bodies to advertise products that had nothing to do with being young, attractive, and unclad. We protested that practice vigorously. Why did half-naked women appear in ads for bulldozers? There was no connection between them! But now young women don't seem to mind becoming such sex objects. Ads are again quite sexually provocative, even when selling something that has nothing to do with sex, like canned green beans.[12]

The amount of skin is not the issue. It is the *differing standards* for skin exposure between women and men that are inappropriate. It does not matter whether women are required to be unduly worried about exposing even a wisp of hair but men do not, or whether women are culturally encouraged to display much more skin than men, for no apparent reason other than to be more provocative. Much more relevant is that clothing needs to be comfortable, functional, and not unduly restricting, for both women and men. For both, that would sometimes involve more skin and sometimes less skin, sometimes skirts and sometimes trousers.

Trading sexual favors has great antiquity, with prostitution often being called "the world's oldest profession." In Buddhism, from antiquity to present-day Western Buddhism, this exchange has also caused a great deal of controversy and heartache. In one canonical narrative, a laywoman donor and a monk are having a mutually satisfying dharma discussion. The woman asks the monk what he needs in the way of provisions, and he replies that the most helpful gift would be something that is hard for monks to obtain—sexual intercourse. The woman prepares to comply, but he changes his mind and becomes verbally abusive to the woman. When this affair is brought to the attention of the Buddha, he castigates the monk severely.[13] Such a story can be multiplied a thousandfold in modern Buddhist circles and has caused major scandals, loss of faith in the dharma, and the censure of teachers who were highly regarded in other ways. At controversy is not whether the sex was consensual; usually it was. But was it appropriate? Later in their lives, women who participated in such affairs will claim that they were taken advantage of by the men involved. But some such women will also admit that low self-esteem led them into "slutty" behavior (their words, not mine), by which they usually mean that they were quite promiscuous when they were younger and had the opportunity. Some of my women Buddhist age-peers have also told me that, as we all became older, they began to appreciate what I was saying as a feminist for the first time. Before that, they told me, they were enjoying their sexual power over men too much to worry about male dominance and what it was doing to them in the long term!

In my estimation, these situations are difficult to evaluate. Certainly women enjoy sex as much as men, and there is no reason why we should be more restricted sexually than men. Fertility control is the responsibility of both women and men. And women must be allowed to make their own decisions and their own mistakes. I am not in favor of rules that unduly restrict mature women's sexual choices and behaviors. Otherwise it is nonsensical to talk about women's equality or freedom. However, dignity and emotional well-being also require proper restraint, as much for men as for women. A man can also be a "slut." If there is blame to be meted out, in this case it goes back to the early messages that instill low self-esteem in girls by making it clear to them that they are less valued than boys. The more that message takes, the more girls and women become addicted to men and to relationships with men as the panacea to all their problems. Of course, such neediness never works well in the long run. The only solution to women's being complicit in becoming sex objects is socializing girls to value themselves as human beings rather than to need male approval so desperately. So long as girls learn early on that they are less valued than their brothers and that their route to success lies in gaining male affection and approval, we can expect a great deal of inappropriately "slutty" behavior on the part of women, at least so long as they are able to garner that approval through sex. Seeking and needing male approval is the great downfall of the typical ego style of a woman caught in the prison of patriarchal gender roles. And since patriarchal men often prefer less competent to more competent women, women comply with their requests by self-diminishment, especially during the years when it is most important for them to become confident and competent in their own right.

THE MOTHER ROLE AND ITS MODERN LIMITS

As is already clear, the obligation to mother, to take care of men and children, ranks high in accounts of how the prison of gender roles affects women. However, much more information is available about how others, especially men, think that women should feel about those obligations and how important they should be to women. We know much less about how women themselves feel about these obligations, because first-person accounts from women, especially historical accounts, are quite rare. There are some famous stories and some stereotypes, but little else. Because most Buddhist literature comes from the literate elite, from monastics and not householders, we are much more likely to hear about or from women who renounced motherhood for one reason or another, rather than from those who found their assigned role satisfying.

Nevertheless, throughout Buddhist history, most Buddhist women have become mothers. For married women without birth control, such an outcome was almost certain. While the option to become a nun was technically available, in most Buddhist cultures, monasticism was far more acceptable for men than for women. If a son became a monk, that brought prestige to a family, while having a daughter become a nun did not, and monks were better supported economically and better educated than were nuns. Because monastics were so dependent on female lay donors for their everyday needs, they greatly preferred that women be pious, generous lay donors than that they be nuns. In terms of receiving social approval, a woman's best option was to become a mother—but the mother of sons, not just a mother. She would also receive approval for encouraging her son to become a monastic, and in many ways, in her role as lay donor, she became a mother to the sangha in general.[14] While filling that role, a woman was expected to display the paramount Buddhist qualities of virtue and wisdom. Filling the wife-and-mother role well would lead to future positive rebirth on the long path to eventual liberation, but it does not lead directly to enlightenment (that is also the case with parenthood for men).

Among the many stories about mothers found in Buddhist literature, most of the more distinctive, individualized accounts of motherhood emphasize its sorrowful, negative aspects, not the positive outcomes that are stressed in more abstract, generalized accounts. Many of the women we meet in the *Therigatha*, the songs of the female elders, had been wives and mothers. None of them recalls that life with fondness, and many delight in their newfound freedom from those roles. The grief of attachment to children who die is one motivation for renouncing and one of the most poignant stories is that of Kisa Gotami. Actually two different stories of mothers' grief are attached to that name, but the best known is in Dhammapala's commentary on the *Therigatha*, often translated with the actual *Therigatha* verses.[15] In this famous story, Kisa Gotami, deranged by grief at the death of her son, refuses to let his body be cremated. People trying to help her bring her to the Buddha, and she asks him to cure her son. He tells her that he will, but she must first bring him some mustard seed from a household that has not experienced the death of someone beloved. She is overjoyed that a cure has been promised, but, of course, she is unsuccessful in her search. Insight into impermanence dawns, she puts down her son's body, returns to the Buddha, and becomes a nun and one of his most praised disciples.

A statement from a much later period, found in a Tibetan folk drama set in the eleventh century about a woman named Nangsa Obum, expresses the limitations motherhood often imposed on women. Such folk dramas were popular entertainment, and women in particular identified with the heroine, a woman who eventually found liberation after many trials and adventures. However, early in her life, she was married and had a son, which kept her from leading the life of Buddhist practice she longed for. She cries, while nursing him, "My son, children are like a rope that pulls a woman into samsara."[16] This single utterance captures the feelings of many women who, willy-nilly, probably early in their lives, found themselves becoming wives and mothers. It also captures the common conclusion that ordinary householder life is incompatible with deep Buddhist practice and seems to indicate that these obligations weigh more heavily on mothers than on fathers.

The most famous, and much loved, encomium to motherhood is found in the context of a Buddhist praise of *metta*, universal friendliness, which is a cardinal Buddhist virtue. The text is from the *Sutta Nipata*, and the most frequently quoted verses recommend as follows:

Even as a mother protects with her life
    Her child, her only child,
So with a boundless heart
    Should one cherish all living beings;
Radiating kindness over the entire world:
    Spreading upwards to the skies,
And downwards to the depths;
    Outwards and unbounded,
Freed from hatred and ill-will.
    Whether standing or walking, seated or lying down
Free from drowsiness,
    One should sustain this recollection.[17]

Beautiful as these verses are, a mother's unique love for her only child is a *simile* for how the ideal Buddhist practitioner should regard all beings. This unique love for one's own child could become the germ for developing metta, but simply regarding one's own child with unique love and compassion is not itself metta, something that many commentators overlook when praising mothers.

In fact, even this simile can be turned against women themselves. A woman teacher once explained to me that women so rarely become enlightened because their unique regard for their own children, a form of attachment, is stronger than their cultivation of metta, *universal* friendliness. This sentiment seems to have been fairly common, especially in contexts that praise bodhisattvas for their universal love, which is *contrasted* with mother-love.[18] In those texts, one is to develop love and compassion toward all beings, not in imitation of mother-love, but because all sentient beings have been one's mother at one time or another, and, as one's mothers, have suffered because of their attachment to their own children. Thus, instead of being close to enlightenment, mother-love, if characterized by too much attachment, actually points in the opposite direction—something that few commentators care to acknowledge. The saving grace, given that caring for children is necessary if humans are to survive from generation to generation, is that it is the *attachment*, not the *love*, that causes the problems. This danger could easily be decreased if responsibilities for childcare were more widely shared. Thus, I welcome the innovation made in some English-language Buddhist liturgies to use the phrase "all sentient beings who have been my *parents*," rather than the much more common "all sentient beings who have been my mothers."

However motherhood and the prison of gender roles have been configured in the past, whether in Buddhist or non-Buddhist contexts, at present we are in the midst of a welcome and thoroughgoing revolution regarding traditional versions of the prison of gender roles. Modern medicine in particular requires this revolution, at least if we want to continue to have a life on planet Earth worthy of the Buddhist evaluation that this is a "precious human life." The situation is actually quite simple. Infant and child mortality rates have declined significantly while at the same time longevity has increased significantly. But fertility rates in most of the world have stayed constant or increased. Obviously, population will only increase and continue to increase unless something in that situation changes. Experts on the carrying capacity of the planet calculate that, at a decent standard of living for all, though without complete economic equality, the planet could support about two billion people. That was the Earth's population in 1930.[19] It is estimated that it took two hundred thousand years for human population to reach one billion in 1815 and then over a century for the population to double to two billion in 1930. Since then, in less than one hundred years, it has grown to seven billion, and many fear ten billion before the end of the twenty-first century.[20] At the same time, rates of resource consumption per human being have also increased, and while many decry such high rates of consumption, no one wants to cut their *own* rate of consuming significantly. In fact, most people, including many who criticize high levels of consumption in *other* societies, want their own rate of consumption to increase. Modern technology is attractive to people all over the world, who want automobiles, refrigerators, computers, air travel, and cell phones in increasing numbers. It should not take a great deal of insight to realize that this situation is unsustainable and cannot continue.

Clearly, by prolonging many, many lives, modern medicine has played a large role in these developments. Fortunately, it can also play a large role in the solution, while also doing a great deal to deliver all of us, both women and men, from the prison of gender roles. Because the death rate is now so much lower, women no longer have to spend their entire lifespans being pregnant, giving birth, nursing, and taking care of young children. That excuse for insisting that women not be educated, thus making them unable to participate easily in cultural and spiritual life no longer has validity. Because safe, relatively reliable methods of fertility control are also now readily available, it is entirely possible to easily reverse the trend of disastrous population growth. If the entire world adopted a one-child policy tomorrow, by the end of the twenty-first century, the world's population would return to 1.6 billion, what it was in 1900, a sustainable population with a high standard of living.[21] This drop in population would not involve starvation, warfare, or epidemic disease, things quite likely to curb population in much more unpleasant ways than the use of birth control—but which would ensue if we refuse to use birth control. While a one-child policy is unlikely to be adopted worldwide, reducing population to sustainable levels obviously does require less than the replacement rate of two children per family. Given the strength of human sexual desire, such outcomes would be nearly impossible without birth control. But with birth control, such outcomes would be quite painless. Why would anyone need more than one, or at most, two children under modern conditions in which most children survive into adulthood? Most people would not want to give up the lower death rates for any reason. But there are trade-offs. It is simply impossible to have both lower death rates with increased longevity and unlimited fertility. Which do we want more? Who could possibly choose unlimited fertility over a longer, better life?

Yet probably most people considering this possibility are pessimistic that it could become reality. Why are people so reluctant to take simple steps involving so little pain to themselves but that would help assure a much better future for everyone now alive or yet to be born? The concepts discussed in chapter 2, ignoring and clinging, contain the answer. People routinely ignore facts such as that abstinence-based sex education does not work or that women usually prefer to limit their fertility when they have that option, especially if they are educated and have economic options. Obviously, anybody who reproduces excessively is ignoring the dire consequences likely to be faced by the children they insist on producing. One has to wonder about such parents! Clinging plays an even larger role in people's unwillingness to bring this vision into fruition. "But I want (more) children," some proclaim, completely ignoring the consequences of fulfilling that attachment. Many bow before this demand as if it had incontrovertible moral authority and, unlike virtually every other desire people express longing for, should not be analyzed or subjected to criticism. When I was a young woman in the 1960s and 1970s and expressed my intent not to have any children, I routinely was criticized as "selfish." But what's selfish about not having children in an overpopulated world? Whether I had produced two children or ten children, the world simply doesn't need those bodies. But it does need what I have contributed through my nonreproductive life of scholarship and teaching. Anybody who thinks the world requires their genetic material to survive has a large ego problem. And if they take so much pleasure in rearing children and are so good at it that the world would profit from having them raise more children, there are plenty of abandoned, needy children around the world who could use their help!

We must conclude that the modern medical developments that have led to lowering the death rate significantly, thus increasing longevity, and making birth control possible and easy also *require* significant revisions to long-held assumptions about conventional gender roles. Women's lives have changed dramatically as a result of these modern developments, and these changes require changes in the whole interdependent matrix of gender roles. Unless we want to destroy the planet and our futures, women are not going to *need* to use their whole life energy for reproduction any longer, nor will be they *able* to do so. They live too long for that, and the planet does not need so many children. This is a great blessing for women, who no longer need to spend their whole lives taking care of men and children, the fifth of the five woes of being a woman listed in Buddhist texts from Buddhism's beginnings to the present day. I would go so far as to claim that nothing has ever been a greater boon for women than the development of safe, effective methods of birth control that could easily be available to all. This development could end the prison of gender roles, if people can tame the way they ignore the downside of conventional gender roles and cling to habitual patterns of male-female relationships.

But, from Buddhist understandings of interdependence, we learn that if a single factor in the interdependent matrix changes, other things will change as well. The prison of gender roles must change for men as well, in ways that could be of great benefit to men. Women, who can no longer fulfill their lives' purpose and meaning through reproduction, through taking care of men and children, will replace that task with more meaningful and demanding professional roles, which society now needs more than their lifelong immersion in reproduction. Not only does society in general need women to be more involved in the economy, but their own families now depend on their economic input as well. In short, the career and parenting paths of women and men need to become much more similar to each other. But, as men know, interrupting a work life can have negative consequences for that work life, and the longer the interruption, the more difficult returning to paid employment can be. There is no reason for women only to bear the entire burden of interrupting their professional careers while men are unaffected by changing social needs and women's changing roles. Other solutions need to be found. Men's fear of being feminized manifests not only in their fear of skirts but in their unwillingness to be deeply involved in the daily, routine care of young children. That needs to change, despite widespread prejudice, sometimes expressed to me by women who claim that men simply couldn't do such tasks. Others claim that men simply shouldn't have to do things like change diapers, deal with screaming infants, prepare formula, bathe babies, or simply take the time out of their projects that it takes to socialize children.

It might sound as if women would gain more from these changes than men. Even if that is true, the gains in equity between women and men and in fairness for women would make these changes worthwhile. Additionally, given how much men want children and pressure women into having children or more children, or don't take responsibility for using birth control, including condoms, it is more than fair and appropriate that they share much more equally in the difficulties attendant on having children. We do need to revise the stereotype that it is mainly women who want children. In my experience, both personally and anecdotally, men are invested in fathering children, but they have unrealistic ideas about how time-consuming and disruptive that development will be.

Additionally, however, the Dalai Lama's insights into the benefits women gain by working so closely with young children are applicable to men. As the Dalai Lama has become more vocal in his support of feminism and of bhikshuni ordination, he has also commented on what he sees as positive qualities that are developed by taking on tasks typically associated with the female gender role:

> Perhaps because they carry children in their wombs and have been the primary caretakers of newborn infants, women develop affection and warm-heartedness more easily than men. For this reason, women must take a more central role in society. Of course men and women have equal potential for both affection and aggression.[22]

While men are unlikely to carry children in wombs anytime soon, if being primary caretakers of newborn infants is so beneficial to women, and, therefore, to society as a whole, and if men have an equal potential with women to develop affection, the conclusion would seem to be completely obvious. To quote a folk proverb, "What's sauce for the goose is sauce for the gander." If taking care of newborn infants helps women become more affectionate and warm-hearted, and if, as must be the case, men have equal capacity with women to develop warm-heartedness, then men desperately need to take on that task. The development in men of more affection and warm-heartedness would be so helpful, both for men themselves and for overall social well-being. Nothing is more vital or would contribute more to global well-being than that men become less predisposed to aggression, competition, violence, and warfare.

Thinking about the value of mother-love and nurturing to society as a whole needs to be extended in another way. Many activities in addition to taking care of one's own children should be considered to be nurturing activities and valued as such. It causes great social harm that they are not so regarded. Limiting what we think of as nurturance only to women taking care of their own children is extremely inadequate. Most people do recognize that nurturing is valuable and necessary and feel kindly disposed toward those who do it. Why do teachers, police officers, professors, authors, artists, health care workers, and people who work in service professions not receive the same affection and respect, given that their work is just as necessary and as socially useful as taking care of one's own children? Such people do a great deal to nurture the entire matrix in which our lives take place, if they are to take place in a satisfactory way. Buddhist ethics included the category of "right livelihood," which for lay practitioners means obtaining one's livelihood in ways that do not cause harm to anyone or to society in general. Any activity that could qualify as "right livelihood" could profitably be thought of as a nurturing role. Those who engage in such activities should be regarded with the same approval, affection, and kindness we generally extend to those whom we regard as nurturers.

Twentieth-century second-wave feminists produced extremely cogent analysis of the downside of the traditional woman-monopolized mother-role as it had come to be constructed by the mid-twentieth century, at least in the American middle class that so many longed to emulate. Anyone who feels nostalgia for the "good old days" of traditional gender roles would do well to take their comments seriously. The norm and ideal was for men to be solely burdened with the work of "breadwinning." Anything less was a threat to their masculinity. Women were solely burdened with the work of childcare and housework, which, it was said, would give them complete emotional fulfillment. They needed no intellectual, spiritual, or cultural involvement in addition to what their mothering and housework would provide them. A man who fulfilled his role properly provided a house in the suburbs, far from the cultural and social activities found in cities and usually without public transportation. There women were isolated with their biological children, rarely seeing other adults, except for husbands who came home after working long hours, wanting to relax. Children had few other adults with whom to interact regularly, which made for intense and often difficult mother-child relationships. Women such as Betty Friedan and Adrienne Rich who wrote about why this lifestyle was so unsatisfying often referenced the boredom and loneliness of so little adult companionship. Though I did not grow up in that kind of middle-class environment, the whole picture was clear to me as a girl socialized in the 1950s at the height of this version of the prison of gender roles. No wonder I so much dreaded having to participate in it myself and did everything I could to avoid that fate.

Of all the analyses of the problems inherent in traditional versions of the prison of gender roles, none is more cogent than Dorothy Dinnerstein's *The Mermaid and the Minotaur*, originally published in 1978. Initially, that book was commented on a great deal, but it has not been discussed much in recent years, which I evaluate as a mistake and a great loss. Dinnerstein's central thesis is about the need for joint parenting if we are to overcome major social problems and produce adults who are more emotionally balanced and healthy. Joint parenting would free women to have more time for other pursuits, but the fairness of that arrangement is only one of its many benefits.

As Dinnerstein sees it—and I think her view accords with Buddhist analyses—infancy and early childhood are not especially pleasant or easy times for the child, who is being introduced to what we Buddhists call "samsara," the limits and frustrations of life. *Nothing* a parent does, no quality of care, no matter how appropriate and loving, can alter or change this basic fact, which is disturbing to both parent and child. In this drama of guilt and blame, says Dinnerstein,

> Mother is the source of pleasure and pain for the infant, who is never certain whether his or her physical or psychological needs will be met. As a result, the infant grows up feeling very ambivalent toward mother figures (women) and what they represent (the material/physical universe).[23]

Thus, mothers come in for more resentment than fathers because, as Dinnerstein sees it, in a culture that places on women alone primary responsibility for childcare, women preside over all the incidents of frustration and limitation that initiate us into the human condition, and are subconsciously blamed for those inevitabilities in a way that men are not—even if (returning to our Buddhist context) the child later learns that such suffering is inevitable and results from karma accrued in past lives.

For Buddhists, however, introduction to samsara is not the only message we learn. Only the first two of the Four Noble Truths talk about samsara. The last two talk about release, freedom, and spiritual discipline. But under traditional gender arrangements, the gurus and religious teachers who introduce us to those disciplines and to the possibility of nirvana are almost always men. This sexual division of labor, in which only women initiate us to samsara but only men introduce us to spiritual disciplines and the possibility of freedom, is difficult and unbalanced. Women have generally been excluded from religious leadership and from teaching roles in Buddhism, but they alone are left with the task of introducing their children to samsara, while men are freed both to pursue nirvana for themselves and to teach the methods promoting freedom to others. The other side of breaking out of the prison of gender roles involves not only men's taking up their fair share of the responsibilities for infant and child care but also women's becoming competent and able to take up the role of being a Buddhist teacher.

According to Dinnerstein, if women are the only ones who bring unpleasant messages to infants, then men, when grown, don't want to reexperience such utter dependence on another, and they seek to control both women and nature. Women, when grown, seek to be controlled by men, trying to keep their own maternal power in check. Most important, women's control over child-rearing is responsible for "our subsequent tendency to blame mother/woman for everything wrong with the human condition, especially the fact that we are limited beings destined to fail and ultimately to die."[24] This "mother-blaming" could be rectified by dual parenting. Because men would share equally in the task of nurturing infants and introducing them to the frustrations of being human, grown-up infants—that is, adults—will no longer be able to scapegoat women and blame them alone for the human condition. Therefore, the major reason for dual parenting is not to free women to participate more fully in culture or to allow men to experience the satisfactions of parenthood, though these are useful side effects. The critical need served by dual parenting is to free the next generation from the unconscious hatred and fear of women that makes mutually satisfying relations between the sexes, as well as full humanity, so difficult for both women and men to achieve.

Though Dinnerstein's analysis rings true to me, when teaching her theses, I have encountered a great deal of resistance from students, who claim that they don't feel any ambivalence or resentment toward their mothers. Many things could explain their impressions. Perhaps those memories have slipped from conscious awareness, which is not uncommon, or perhaps their mothers had more extensive childcare networks or weren't as frustrated as some mothers who don't enjoy caring for infants and young children as much as other parents may. I, however, do remember being a terrified young child who had no idea what I was doing to displease my mother but expected to be scolded or swatted a few times and tried to anticipate what I could do differently. As I approached adulthood, I once complained to my mother that she had tried to break my spirit when I was young. She replied by confessing that she had not enjoyed having to take care of a baby or young child much. Assigned conventional gender roles are often cruel and dysfunctional for all concerned.

Student disclaimers about Dinnerstein's thesis aside, I suggest that it gives a cogent explanation of two phenomena that are otherwise difficult to explain. Why do we experience such an epidemic of mother-blaming and criticisms of our own mothers these days? Virtually everyone has a major story about frustration and dissatisfaction with their mother that are completely unparalleled by similar dissatisfactions with and stories about their father. Could it be explained by too much mother presence and a great deal of father absence, even in two-parent families, which are somewhat rare? Why is there so much misogyny and violence toward birth givers in so many cultures and religions? All living beings owe their life to a female birth giver. Nevertheless, in so many religious texts, even Buddhist texts, extreme fear and hatred of women and disgust with their bodies are freely and frequently expressed. Misogyny and violence toward women make no sense if patriarchal men actually revere mothers as much as they claim to, especially when they tell us that the reverence we receive as mothers should be all we need in our lives.

Because of feminism's limited success, such remarks are now much less common than they used to be. I remember well a time when complaining about women and making disparaging remarks about women were commonplace and when objections to such comments brought disapproval. Comments that trivialize and are hostile to feminism, the movement to promote dignity and equality for women, are part of that package. I also remember being ridiculed by men, some of them Asian Buddhist men, for being a feminist who didn't understand, according to them, that in Asia mothers are revered. They must have thought I didn't know about the misogyny in Asian Buddhist texts or about women's limited roles. It is not possible to revere mothers enough to atone for all the misogyny and violence that has been visited upon women. Nor could motherhood alone be sufficient to realize the potential inherent in having the precious human body so valued by Buddhists.

PARENT AS MOTHER/FATHER? BUDDHIST PERSPECTIVES

Buddhist texts display a clear understanding that a child is the genetic product equally of both parents, even though the term "genes" is not found in those texts. In her excellent 2015 survey, *Women in Pali Buddhism*, Pascale Engelmajer points out that parents are routinely referred to as a compound unit, *matapitaro*, in Buddhist texts and that they head the lists of social hierarchies and those to whom one owes debts.[25] It is frequently said that one could never really fulfill one's obligations to both mother and father, no matter what one did:

> Even if one should carry about one's mother on one shoulder and one's father on the other, and [while doing so] should have a life span of a hundred years, live for a hundred years; and if one should attend to them by anointing them with balms, by massaging, bathing, and rubbing their limbs, and they even void their urine and excrement there, one still would not have

done enough for one's parents, nor would one have repaid them.[26]

This equivalence of mother and father as well as the primacy of parents is also seen in the list found in the Pali Canon of the five heinous deeds, whose karmic impact is formidable to overcome. The list includes patricide and matricide equally as two of the five heinous actions. Parents, both parents, are owed respect similar to that given to the Buddha, dharma, and sangha.[27]

Ideas about the equivalent contribution of each parent carry through in much later materials found in esoteric Vajrayana teachings about the subtle body and how it comes into being through the process of conception and dissolves again at death. According to these teachings, each person inherits the "red element" of wisdom and emptiness from the mother while inheriting the "white element" of compassion (or skillful means) and form from the father. At conception these two come together and separately move to opposite ends of the central channel of the subtle body, where they remain throughout one's life. As death occurs, they again merge in the heart center.[28] In this context, speculations about Vajrayana esotericism are not the point. The point is that in tantric complementary dyadic symbolism, the nonduality of form and emptiness, and of wisdom and skillful means/compassion, are the keys that unlock the entire puzzle of what is important, of how things really are. Everyone, without distinction as to whether they are a man or a woman, is the result of the presence of both the red and the white elements in their being. These elements are equally constitutive of the person, and each parent contributes his or her equally equivalent element.

By contrast, founding narratives in Western culture regard the male as the true parent, with the female being only a passive container in which the new being contained in the semen grows. This view of the relative contributions of male and female to the new child dominated Western thinking until the seventeenth century, when one of the first uses of the newly discovered microscope was to observe sperm in semen, which was declared to empirically prove "Aristotle's intuition 'that it is exclusively the male semen which forms the fetus, and that all that the woman may contribute only serves to receive the semen and feed it.'"[29] A colleague of mine reported that in nursing education classrooms in twentieth-century North America, she still encountered students who were surprised to learn that the male's semen did not contain the entire new child.

This view can be traced to both roots of Western culture, the Greeks and the Hebrews, though it is more explicit in the Greek heritage. In addition to Aristotle's influence, some of the most important Greek tragedies "solved" the issue of who was the "true parent." In *The Furies*, Aeschylus penned the famous lines: "The mother is no parent of that which is called her child, but only nurse of the new-planted seed that grows. The parent is he who mounts. A stranger, she preserves a stranger's seed."[30] The context for these lines was a dispute over which is the worse crime, matricide or patricide. It was decided that patricide is worse because the father is the true parent. The "proof" for this claim is that the Greek god Zeus created the goddess Athena without the aid of a female parent, whereas females could not produce a child without the aid of a male parent. The biblical myth of Eve's creation out of Adam's rib, which has such deep impact on Western views that women are secondary, subservient beings, makes much the same point, though Eve is not created by Adam but by the male creator god. (It should be noted in passing that this male-dominant interpretation of the biblical story of the creation of humanity is deeply flawed. Much less male-dominant interpretations are easily possible, but they have never taken hold in Western imagination.)

Clearly these Western views on the relative value of the male or the female parent contrast significantly with Buddhist views, which emphasize the equal debt one owes to both mother and father and the equality of matricide and patricide as crimes. For Western Buddhists, clearly the Buddhist emphasis on the fundamental equality of both parents should take precedence over the much more male-dominant Western views. Given that in the Buddhist view, a child has equal obligations to both parents, so also parenting duties would fall equally on each parent, though that point is not made so explicitly in Buddhist texts. The point in this context, in which I am talking about the prison of gender roles in the lives of Western Buddhists, is that the compound of parents as a single unit, exhibited though not sufficiently highlighted in classical Buddhist texts, offers an ideal of both parents being equal and equally important.

But for parents to merit that kind of regard, they have to become a genuine unit, in contrast to many contemporary Western practices. For women and men to have more complementary roles in taking care of their children both as economic providers and as routine caregivers would turn them into a compound unit, as in the Pali compound *matapitaro* mentioned earlier, which doesn't mean "parent" but "mother-father" as one term. Such practices would contrast to situations in which childcare, with all its burdens, is left so completely to women. To warrant the kind of reverence and duty that should be given to fathers according to these Buddhist texts, they would need to be more involved in everyday care in more ways than the "breadwinner" role, something already taking place in many families. But, given modern conditions, it can also be asked that mothers take on the breadwinner role as well, something that happens in most families despite the fact that women don't make equal money for equal work. At this point in time, society and employers do almost nothing to make being a mother-father unit easier to manage.

CONCLUSIONS

Many texts on anthropology and sociology discuss primary gendered tasks as "reproduction" for women and "production" for men. Presumably, there should be some complementarity between the dignity of these various roles and how interesting and rewarding the work connected with each role is. For complementarity to be real, one should be able to make a satisfying, fulfilling life out of either the male or the female role as constituted in any given social construction. It is hard to imagine why people would continue to fulfill their assigned tasks well without such complementarity. One can also assume that there is a "fit" between the assigned gendered tasks and available technology.

However, it is a subtle and sensitive matter to determine when purported "complementarity" devolves into "mutual incompetence." In situations of mutual incompetence, both women and men are assigned limited roles, neither of which is satisfying, though filling those roles keeps "the system" going. That becomes the justification for keeping individuals trapped in their individually unsatisfying mutual incompetence. Given modern technology, a system that keeps women out of meaningful spiritual vocations and professions and men out of significant, daily routine childcare has become a system fostering mutual incompetence— aka, the prison of gender roles.

When thinking about the prison of gender roles, especially in Buddhism, generally it is my preference not to denigrate past solutions to complex problems. There's just no point in being angry about past situations for being as they were. If one understands interdependence, one understands that the past could not have been different than it was. Yes, it is painful to remember that for generations Buddhists have regarded the solution to the problems attendant on birth as a woman to be future rebirth as a man. But today, many technologies, birth control foremost among them, make the prison of gender roles and its mutual incompetence more than obsolete.

In the face of discussions of the prison of gender roles such as I have presented in this chapter, some skeptics claim that there are no problems regarding the prison of gender roles anymore, that it is all a thing of the past. Accompanying this claim is often the supposition that only a few overvigilant women still persist in talking about these old issues. Granted, at least in some Western societies, many situations have changed even within my lifetime. For one thing, in Western Buddhism, about half the dharma teachers are women, a situation unprecedented in Buddhist history. I could no longer ask the question I asked an early teacher of mine, an episode narrated earlier in this chapter. But it would be naive to assume that such recent changes guarantee long-term improvements. Who would ever have thought that we North American women would have to fight to keep birth control and abortion available to us, as we now must in the current "war on women" being waged by conservative American politicians? And birth control is the single item most responsible for the current demise of the prison of gender roles. Without that, everything else is up for question. Don't be so complacent and naive!

FOUR

FREEDOM FROM THE PRISON OF GENDER ROLES

After his enlightenment experience, the historical Buddha is said to have doubted whether he should try to teach what he had discovered. It went so much against the grain of conventional human desires and expectations that he doubted anyone would take his teachings seriously. As someone who has taught Buddhism to hundreds of undergraduates, I have some glimpse into the Buddha's doubts. People just don't want to hear that conventional habits always bring suffering in their wake or that satisfying desires will never bring true happiness. Not being able to hear the rest of the Buddha's teachings, that relief is possible and that there are clear, simple practices that bring relief, they conclude that Buddhism is pessimistic and unrealistic. Resistance to Buddhist teachings is often initially extreme when these teachings are first encountered. Even people who take up Buddhist practices often experience lengthy periods of not really "getting it," of repeatedly encountering the same habitual tendencies and habits that have not worked in the past but prove to be tenacious. Resistance is not something that is only encountered before one begins serious Buddhist practice. It persists for years and years. The historical Buddha was correct that we would find his teachings difficult to assimilate even when we find them convincing and trustworthy. Old habits are only slowly uprooted, but Buddhist teachings do promise that they can be eradicated, which brings relief and freedom.

Because resistance is so persistent and long-lasting, Buddhist training programs recommend serious investigation through meditation and contemplation into the habitual patterns that have brought suffering. This is what Dogen Zenji called "studying the self" so that one could "forget the self." That is the only way to "study the way of enlightenment." There are no real shortcuts. One can't say, "But I don't want to study the self. It's too depressing," or "It's too difficult. I just want to keep all my habitual patterns." One could say that, but one wouldn't get far into the way of enlightenment. So why, if one becomes willing to study the self, would one resist studying the gendered self with the same thoroughness? Our trip through the prison of gender roles, which was nowhere nearly as grim or as long as it could have been, was unpleasant. But without revulsion would we ever develop renunciation of counterproductive painful habitual patterns?[1]

HOW TO STUDY THE SELF: WHAT THE BUDDHA TAUGHT

In early Buddhist texts, the Buddha is often represented as teaching his students to abandon that which we normally take to be the self, but which, ultimately, is not us "not ours." In one such long teaching, as is often the case, the undisciplined student is compared unfavorably with the student who studied the self:

Bhikkhus, an untaught ordinary person, who has no regard for noble ones and is unskilled and undisciplined in their Dhamma, who has no regard for true men and is unskilled and undisciplined in their Dhamma, regards material form thus: "This is mine, this I am, this is my self." He regards perception thus: "This is mine, this I am, this is my self." He regards formations thus: "This is mine, this I am, this is my self." He regards feeling thus: "This is mine, this I am, this is my self." He regards what is seen, heard, sensed, cognized, encountered, sought, mentally pondered thus: "This is mine, this I am, this is my self." . . .

Bhikkhus, a well-taught noble disciple who has regard for noble ones and is skilled and disciplined in their Dhamma, who has regard for true men and is skilled and disciplined in their Dhamma, regards material form thus: "This is not mine, this I am not, this is not my self." He regards feeling thus: "This is not mine, this I am not, this is not my self." He regards perception thus: "This is not mine, this I am not, this is not my self." He regards formations thus: "This is not mine, this I am not, this is not my self." He regards what is seen, heard, sensed, cognized, encountered, sought, mentally pondered thus: "This is not mine, this I am not, this is not my self." [2]

The student who has truly studied the self does not confuse anything one experiences through the five skandhas or the six senses as being the basis of an enduring self, because she realizes that none of them can rise to the standard of being reliable and enduring, rather than ephemeral—that none of them can provide true happiness.

The reason to study the self so closely? Many other early teachings link abandoning what is not truly one's own with welfare and happiness:

> Bhikkhus, whatever is not yours, abandon it. When you have abandoned it, that will lead to your welfare and happiness. And what is it, bhikkhus, that is not yours? Form is not yours, abandon it. . . . Feeling is not yours. . . . Perception is not yours. . . . Volitional formations are not yours. . . . Consciousness in not yours. When you have abandoned it, that will lead to your welfare and happiness. [3]

Such teaching is widespread: these are normal Buddhist teachings, rewritten and reworded in many words and many texts, in all schools of Buddhism throughout all Buddhist history.

People sometimes become impatient with my emphases on Buddhism and gender, asking me, "What does all this gender talk have to do with real dharma?" Every feeling, perception, volitional formation, experience, or thought through which the prison of gender roles is constructed and maintained is easily subsumed within any and all of the categories that the Buddha discusses in the above teachings. In fact, they are the way the five skandhas, and so on, of ego-grasping are most likely to be encountered in everyday life, which is where we have to stop thinking they are "ours." By becoming attached to these gender conventions, by letting them dictate our lives, we lose our welfare and happiness just as surely as if we believe that our experiences of form, feelings, any of our thoughts, and so forth, have true reality. Anyone who wants to progress in studying the self must disown those things that seem so real to us, especially our thoughts, beliefs, and ideologies. Many "untaught ordinary persons" believe just as deeply in their assumptions and ideologies about gender as they believe in the reality of their forms, perceptions, and the like. In fact, often they are more certain about gender than any other aspect of what seems to them to be "theirs." So what better place to begin to study the self than with what seems most real, most certainly relevant about that purported self to the "untaught, ordinary" person? Especially given that the attachments of which we are not even aware bind us the most tightly. That is how we remain unable to forget the self, no matter how much we want to. Such advice applies to Buddhists who claim to believe in egolessness but claim that gender issues have nothing to do with dharma, even while they continue to cling to the gender norms current in their society or class.

Such a person who happens to have a penis may conclude that such a body part means something incontrovertible, something real and true. "I'm a man, therefore I should have social dominance, because no matter where I rank in hierarchies among men, at least I'm better than any woman, and any woman who is competent makes me uncomfortable. My body parts and hers mean that she can't be a nun, shouldn't be educated, and should devote her life, first and foremost, to taking care of me and my children." If such a person took Buddhist advice seriously, he would immediately reflect, "These thoughts and perceptions, even this form, 'is not me, is not mine.' Therefore, I will abandon them, which will be for 'welfare and happiness.'" Women bound in the prison of gender roles, of course, are subject to the reverse thoughts and conclusions about their own forms, their own body parts, and need to do the contemplations appropriate to their own immersion in the prison of gender roles. How could Buddhists who claim that enlightened mind is beyond gender dismiss or disparage those who point out how easily people miss that enlightened mind by taking limited aspects of its relative existence so seriously? What does all this "gender talk" have to do with "real dharma"? Everything! "Gender talk" is not fundamentally a project of social liberation, though it also facilitates social liberation. It is an extremely close and deep way of studying the self, which, we are told, is the only way to forget the self and thus attain "the way of enlightenment." Therefore, I conclude that all the Buddhists who claimed they believed in egolessness but were better Buddhists than me because they had no issues with conventional gender arrangements simply had never taken seriously the Buddha's instruction about every conditioned phenomenon, "This is not mine, this I am not, this is not my self." "When you have abandoned it, that will lead to your welfare and happiness."

The relevance of such exercises is not limited only to those clinging to gender identity. They easily and readily apply to any identity that threatens to overwhelm one, to take over completely one's sense of who one is, any identity to which one is beginning to be attached, any cause to which one gives unconditioned, ultimate loyalty. That comment applies equally to identity as a feminist, a point of which I am more than well aware. Given that Buddhist teachers give this advice even about one's Buddhist identity, obviously it applies to all other causes and identities. In this age of identity politics, of extreme elevation of multiple identities including a multitude of gender-based identities, this Buddhist advice to deconstruct identity step by step, to study the self—whatever form it may have taken—is more than relevant. This point is also helpful when dealing with the ways in which differing movements for human liberation often compete, a question to which I will return in chapter 6.

Such radical relativizing of causes and identities that so many people take so seriously is a difficult discipline. That is why the historical Buddha hesitated to teach it. How does one find one's way in the relative world when nothing in it offers complete security or certainty? That is also a difficult question, to which we will turn before the end of this chapter.

ARE WOMEN AND MEN FUNDAMENTALLY DIFFERENT? BUDDHIST VIEWS

One of the most common and angriest responses to the suggestion that it is important to break free of the prison of gender roles is "But men and women are different!" Well, yes, their bodies look different. Men inseminate and women give birth! But does that say anything about the intellects, minds, and spirits of either, unless we combine those biological differences with a socially created prison of gender roles? How could we possibly deduce from these biological facts that men should dominate women and that men should be freed from time-consuming, repetitive domestic tasks so that they have time for Buddhist study and practice? How do they justify the gender-role assignment that women should spend all their time and energy taking care of men and children, one of the five woes of having a female body identified in many Buddhist texts? How could it possibly translate into justifying conventional, male-dominated gender roles as appropriate? In my own experience, this frequent taunt about differences between men and women usually masks a strident, but unstated, belief that conventional samsaric gender roles are right and good, not to be resisted or tampered with. People have claimed that it is "ideological" of me to object to conventional gender roles. But isn't it at least as ideological to keep insisting on conventional gender roles, which have nothing to recommend them except that they are familiar and conventional? Conventional practices rarely reflect or encourage the enlightened state of mind beyond gender, neither male nor female.

Given how frequently this claim and its attendant justification for conventional gender roles surface among Western Buddhists, it is worthwhile to investigate whether Buddhist texts actually back up these assertions. Of course, one can find texts that back up these more conventional claims. But there is a significant body of Buddhist literature, much less noted by Western Buddhists and, as far as I can tell, also less noted by Asian Buddhists, that would lead one to significantly different conclusions.

As is well known, there is no creation story, per se, in Buddhism, no story of a time before there was something and how the world then came out of nothing. There is, however, a story of how humans came to be as they currently are from an earlier condition in which there were no gender signs and "people" were able to subsist on spontaneously appearing food that required no work. However, people gradually began to develop greed and clinging (*tanha*) regarding this spontaneously appearing food and began to hoard and store it. Their bodies changed, becoming "coarser," and they began to differentiate between those who were more attractive and less attractive. This kind of cycle went through many evolutions until finally, as bodies became coarser and coarser,

> the females developed female sex-organs, and the males developed male organs. And the women became extremely preoccupied with men, and the men with women. Owing to this excessive preoccupation with each other, passion was aroused and their bodies burnt with lust.[4]

This story is crucially important for its differences from the key Western narrative about how humanity came into being. In the Buddhist story, women and men appear simultaneously and become attracted to each other. Neither is at fault for the development of sexual lust.

In the main Western narrative, as usually interpreted, first a male creature is made. Then from him, a female is drawn out. In the Western story, the male is primary and the female is a secondary creature who was made to serve his needs, which is the dominant interpretation of this story. Freud's view of women as incomplete and inadequate castrated human beings is a direct descendent of this biblical story, which dominates Western culture. To make things even worse, the female is routinely blamed for the eventual "fall." That Eve misled Adam into eating the apple has been used for centuries to justify not letting women speak in public or at religious gatherings. Because a woman taught once and got it all wrong, causing humanity's fall, better never to let women have any teaching role in the future!

This story has deeply imprinted itself in Western egos, whether or not people believe in it or are traditionally religious. Its effects on women have been profound and extremely negative. Its modern fallout is the deep androcentrism of Western culture and scholarship, the view that men represent the normal and ideal human, with women being the exception to the norm, but not able to meet that ideal norm. It is behind a common Western view that women "think with their glands," which makes their thinking untrustworthy. Men's thinking, by contrast, they claim, results in a correct view of the world because men's bodies are regarded as providing a normal, direct connection with the world around them—an assumption that conveniently ignores the extent to which men's bodies are also governed by hormones.[5] Thus it is justified to conflate "mankind" and "humanity," claiming that the same word adequately represents both males and all humans. But since women cannot be "men," how could they be included among "all men"? In fact, usually we are not.

Instead of the Western generic masculine, Buddhist texts often use the phrase "whether a man or a woman," which is common in all five *nikayas* of the Pali Canon and in commentaries.[6] This usage

> supports the attitude . . . that insists on including women on a par with men. . . . The metaphors and examples depict a world in which both men and women constituted humankind; women are not subsumed in an overarching "Man." Drawing on another contemporary example, it echoes the resolutely non-androcentric (albeit stylistically inelegant) practice of using the phrase "he or she" when speaking in general about men and women rather than using the (supposedly) inclusive masculine.[7]

In the Buddhist story, humanity is fundamentally "bi-sexed." The two sexes arise together and are more similar than different, as we shall see below. It makes no sense to see one as prior to or more important than the other, as is so often done when interpreting the Western story. To use the term "mankind" for this fundamentally "two-sexed" humanity is clearly inappropriate. Given the stark differences between the Buddhist story of the origin of sexuality and the Western story, Buddhists should always use language that accurately reflects the two-sexed nature of humanity, so that Buddhists, especially Western Buddhists, do not think the Buddhist view of human two-sexed beings shares anything in common with the biblical narrative and the way it makes women derivative, secondary beings, an add-on or afterthought. Generic masculine usage simply cannot carry the burden of communicating that humanity is actually two sexed. Generic masculine language seriously distorts fundamental Buddhist understandings of how women and men are related to each other. For my entire life as a Buddhist scholar-practitioner, I have argued against the common tendency to use generic masculine language in English-language Buddhist liturgies, because it so fundamentally distorts Buddhist insight into the two-sexed nature of humanity. It is incomprehensible to me that Buddhists would resist this linguistic reform, and I have never heard a cogent defense of using generic masculine language in English-language Buddhist liturgies.

That it is initially disrupting to switch from generic masculine to gender-inclusive English-language usage is irrelevant. In the middle to late 1970s, I undertook a deliberate effort to retrain myself in how I used the English language. For example, I made it a point to routinely say "letter carrier," not "mailman." These days, many letter carriers are in fact women, so the new usage is more accurate. It only took a few months for this change to take hold, and the benefits far outweigh any small difficulty. But those who retain gender advantage from using conventional forms still resist. Sometime in the middle 1980s, I was asked to edit a well-used textbook on world religions to get rid of its generic masculine language. The publishers had received multiple complaints about the generic masculine usage and had asked the authors of the various chapters, most of whom were well-known male scholars, to revise their chapters. The authors claimed that they simply did not know how to write using gender-inclusive language, a rather feeble claim coming from people who are competent enough to become well-known scholars. I was already a known scholar in my own right and was working on my own scholarly projects. I declined the invitation, but have always seen it as indicative of how blind people are to male privilege. An up-and-coming younger female scholar should interrupt her work to clean up after well-known male scholars! Why would anyone even think it would be appropriate to make such a request?

In the Buddhist narrative, after human beings become two-sexed, sexuality affects men and women in the same ways, according to some important texts. These texts are also important for their contrast with Western understandings of sexual attraction. In a series of comments, identical claims are made about women and men. These texts contrast in an interesting way with a common pattern of early Buddhist texts in which a student who is undisciplined is contrasted negatively with the student who is studying the self well. Both sets of texts use exactly the same formulae, in the first case regarding men and women and in the second case, the disciplined and the undisciplined student. Exactly the same thing is said about women and men, but the behavior of the undisciplined student is the opposite of the behavior of the disciplined student.

First of all, sexual attraction is described exactly the same way for women and men. The Buddha is represented as having said,

> I do not see even one other form that so obsesses the mind of a man as the form of a woman. The form of a woman obsesses the mind of a man.
>
> I do not see even one other sound that so obsesses the mind of a man as the sound of a woman. . . .
>
> I do not see even one other odor that so obsesses the mind of man as the odor of a woman. . . .
>
> I do not see even one other taste that so obsesses the mind of a man as the taste of a woman. . . .

I do not see even one touch that so obsesses the mind of a man as the touch of a woman.[8]

Then he goes on to say the same thing about how the mind of a woman is affected when her five senses encounter a man: "I do not see even one form that so obsesses the mind of a woman as the form of a man"—and so on.[9]

In another parallel set of passages, both women and men are told that their attachment to their own gender role must be given up— in other words, they need to stop clinging to their specific gender identities. Again, the wording is exactly the same for women and for men. This is a highly abbreviated form of the text as it pertains to men:

> A man, bhikkhus, attends internally to his masculine faculty, his masculine comportment, his masculine appearance, his masculine aspect, his masculine desire, his masculine voice, his masculine ornamentation. He becomes excited by these and takes delight in them. . . . It is in this way that a man does not transcend his masculinity.
>
> A man, bhikkhus, does not attend internally to his masculine faculty . . . his masculine ornamentation. He does not become excited by these nor take delight in them. . . . It is in this way that a man transcends his masculinity.[10]

Clearly, these texts make the point that it is preferable, more liberating, for both men and women to transcend their masculinity and femininity than to remain locked within those gender roles.

The above texts indicate that women and men experience sexual attraction in the same way and with the same intensity. Nevertheless, in many Western accounts of early Indian Buddhism one gets the impression that early Buddhists saw women as more oversexed than men, though more recent scholarship offers correctives to this impression. These differing impressions of how women are represented in early Buddhist literature is part of the androcentric outlook many Western scholars brought to their study of Buddhism.

(This topic will be dealt with more fully in chapter 5.) Texts that represent women as extremely oversexed can easily be found. The Western scholars did not make them up. One of the more notorious of these texts declares, "Bhikkhus, women die unsatisfied and discontent in two things. What two? Sexual intercourse and giving birth. Women die unsatisfied and discontent in these two things."[11]

Another frequently quoted text gave rise to one of the most famous stereotypes about women, that women are "a snare of Mara." The most commonly quoted translation reads as follows:

> Monks, a woman, even when going along, will stop to entice the heart of a man, whether standing, sitting, lying down, laughing, speaking, singing, weeping, stricken, or dying, she will stop to entice the heart of a man. Monks, if it is right to say of anything, "this is wholly a snare of Mara," then it is right to say of womankind, "this is wholly a snare of Mara."[12]

According to this translation, women take the active, seducing role. But a more recent translation by the American Theravada monk Bhikkhu Bodhi puts a different spin on this oft-quoted passage. This passage takes place in the context of discussing a case in which a mother and son, both of whom were monastics, committed incest. During that discussion, the Buddha is represented as saying, "Beings who are lustful for the form of a woman—ravenous, tied to it, infatuated, and blindly absorbed in it—sorrow for a long time under the control of a woman's form"—then he goes on to the idea in the passage quoted above, emphasizing that "the woman obsesses the mind of a man" and so forth.[13] Bhikkhu Bodhi's translation emphasizes that the male is obsessed, which is different from claiming that the female is actively attempting to lure a man into a sexual encounter.

Because Buddhism supports male monasticism so much more fully than female monasticism, the sheer preponderance of texts that discuss problems of sexual attraction for monastics are far more likely to discuss how troublesome women are for monks than vice versa. Especially when combined with translations that portray women as the instigators of this dance of seduction, it could be easy to draw the conclusion that early Buddhists saw women as problematic, and that early Buddhists mainly blamed women for men's attraction to them. This conclusion could more easily be drawn by scholars who themselves have an androcentric mindset, predisposing them to select and interpret data in ways that diminish women and are somewhat hostile to women. But sexual attraction operates in the same way for women and men. Women try to seduce men, but men also try to seduce women. There are many fewer stories in Buddhist literature of male attempts to seduce female monastics, but they are found. In the *Therigatha*, the songs of the female elders, Mara takes on that job himself, rather than sending ordinary men to try. In a contribution to the 2013 book *Women in Early Indian Buddhism*, Bhikkhu Analayo has analyzed these stories and concludes that, far from being weak and easily seduced, these nuns are more often capable than monks in recognizing Mara and dispatching him.[14]

These parallel accounts of male and female attempts at sexual aggression warrant Alice Collett's conclusion in her own study of the implications of stories about how monastic rules governing sexual infractions on the part of monks and nuns came into existence. Rather than drawing the conclusion that women are the initiators, the seducers, she draws the conclusion that "male sexuality is represented as aggressive, potent, and proactive, while female sexuality is passive and responsive" and goes on to say,

Rather than the rules and origin stories revealing women with voracious sexual appetites who are intent upon as much sexual activity as possible, whenever and with whomever they can, it is instead the men's attempts to persuade, cajole, and manipulate women into sex acts with them that stand out.[15]

To continue discussions of how, although human beings are sexed, men and women are not essentially different, we can examine the *abhidharma*, or philosophical teachings, which are the third of the three categories of Buddhist scriptures.[16] The abhidharma contains by far the most complex and detailed teachings in the early, pre-Mahayana Buddhist world. There are two earlier abhidharmas, the Theravada abhidharma, which is still normative for Theravada Buddhists, and the Sarvastivada abhidharma, which was an important basis for much of later Buddhist Mahayana thinking. However, on the topic of innate sexual differences, the two abhidharmas are quite similar. To quote the Pali *Vishuddhimagga* (a fifth-century Theravada text) when discussing the twenty-four kinds of derived materiality that partially comprise the form aggregate or form skandha, the masculine and feminine faculty are described as follows:

> The *femininity faculty* has the female sex as its characteristic. Its function is to show "this is a female." It is manifested as the reason for the mark, sign, work, and ways of the female.
> The *masculinity faculty* has the male sex as its characteristic. Its function is to show "this is a male." It is manifested as the reason for the mark, sign, work, and ways of the male.[17]

It is important to note that nothing different is specified for males and females. They just each have the highly visible gender marker. The Sarvastivada abhidharma makes the same point.

The Sarvastivada texts have a detailed description of the whole Buddhist path. They claim that no one can attain enlightenment in a single birth. It will take at least three lifetimes. A woman can attain the preparatory stages of the path with the same facility as a man, but in the future she will be reborn with the masculine faculty.[18] The texts offer no explanation as to why a woman could not move further on the path while in a female body. This must be one of the doctrinal sources of the widespread popular belief that a woman cannot attain enlightenment. But in this system, almost no one is going to attain enlightenment in their present bodies in any case. At most, a female body could indicate that this person will not attain enlightenment in their present body. Beyond that, however, gender roles are not specified, and it seems that a woman could as readily as a man actually make the all-important breakthrough to the stage of the path from which irreversibly forward movement is guaranteed, unless she is hampered more than men by gender roles that limit her ability to study and practice.

In this detailed description of a gradual path to enlightenment, all reliance on or attention to these faculties or marks eventually must be given up entirely. In both Theravada and Sarvastivada abhidharma, the final approach to realization involves "the signless, the wishless, and emptiness." At this stage of the path, one recognizes definitively that nothing has any inherent being, there is nothing to be desired, and all conventional signs disappear into meaninglessness—including, of course, the masculine and feminine faculties. Conventional existence had been characterized by attributing real existence to relative factors, to wanting things to be one way or another, and by relying on the differentiations provided by different signs or markers. All this must be left behind, according to the texts: "Since they are empty, they are neither male nor female. As for the identity and difference, these are only names which are valid in the hypothesis of 'self' and 'mine.' This is why male and female, identity and difference are really non-existent."[19] Or as the scholar Pascale Engelmajer has put it, "In an ultimate sense, woman and man are concepts that are non-existent and established by convention."[20] Thus, we see early dharmic basis for the claim that gender is irrelevant, that the enlightened mind is neither male nor female.

In a cultural context in which some have gender privilege because of their specific gender marker of masculinity, it is arrogant for those with gender privilege to use that claim to trivialize criticisms from those who lack gender privilege by claiming that enlightened mind is beyond gender, neither male nor female. Instead they should demonstrate that they have transcended their own gender privilege. For that truly dharmic claim to have any real significance, there has to be some recognition of the limits and relativity of any specific system of gender roles. In my experience, those most vociferously proclaiming that I shouldn't be concerned with gender issues because enlightened mind is beyond gender have usually been men, lecturing me with great pomposity and authoritativeness They have thereby demonstrated that they expect to be deferred to only because they are men. But they don't seem to have a glimmer of awareness of the relativity of the specific prison of gender roles they were demanding that I respect and adhere to.

This is the old problem of absolutizing the relative. Such advocates of conventionality would say to me, "But you have to respect the relative and live in the relative world." Of course, one cannot argue with that. But one is also required to recognize the relativity of the relative, which means one doesn't raise it to the absolute by insisting on its universal, infallible relevance. Instead, those most likely to make that argument have been men trying to protect their male gender privilege by arguing that a conventional status quo is too sacrosanct to be questioned or changed. In the long run, what does having the faculty of masculinity or femininity mean? These days it doesn't even mean that you can't change the physical marker that got you designated at birth as belonging to one sex or the other. It seems only that one born as a biological male will never carry children in a womb or give birth, and those born as a biological female will never inseminate another female, even if they acquire a penis through surgery. Those limits I'm willing to accept. The rest of any specific prison of gender roles has no validity. It is simply a relative factor, an agreed-upon convention, as words are often evaluated in Buddhist philosophies. The problem is trying to make words or gender practices carry more than that relative weight, as always happens whenever specific gender roles are insisted upon and enforced.

Thus far, I have cited mainly early Buddhist texts, which are foundational for Buddhism throughout its history, to make the case that at a fundamental level, although people are sexed, their specific sexuality does not add up to essential differences between women and men. Another feature of Buddhism, omnipresent in Mahayana and Vajrayana Buddhism, also offers proof that, though people are sexed, they are not essentially different, which means we can locate nothing that characterizes all males but no females, apart from the physiological signs of sex, and, as we have just noted, even those can be transformed. Early Buddhism did not personify virtues or enlightened qualities. The personalities in its narrative are human beings, historical characters, so they are either men or women. That began to change some centuries into Buddhist history.

Eventually, a huge repertoire of personified Buddhist virtues, as well as multiple Buddhas, bodhisattvas, and others, became well known to all Mahayana and Vajrayana practitioners. These personifications of enlightened wisdom are about equally male and female. Their sexual markers are quite clear. No one looking at them would ever wonder whether they are male or female. Despite their clear sexual markers, they do not observe gender roles, which may be the most important observation one could make about them. These female and male personifications do not carry on different activities or manifest in different ways. Both male and female personifications of both wisdom and compassion, the two central Buddhist virtues, are common. Both male and female personifications of Buddhist virtues can be either peaceful and beneficent, or wrathful, even "ugly," as is appropriate for specific circumstances. Because male monotheism is normative in Western cultures, Westerners are quite unfamiliar with such mythic role models or with portrayals of ultimately important religious figures as females.

The fact that these personifications of Buddhist ideals do not observe gender roles makes them relevant role models for their human worshippers, though the implications of this fact have not been widely recognized. On this point, they express the longings of their worshippers not to be so bound by conventional gender roles and stereotypes. In Vajrayana practice, human beings identify with and visualize themselves as these enlightened beings. When one takes these personifications of Buddhist virtues as a personal practice, the gender of the human practitioner is irrelevant. Men visualize themselves as the powerful and free female personifications of enlightened mind, such as Vajrayogini, or the compassionate, ever-helpful female Tara. Women do these practices in exactly the same way. Women visualize themselves as the peaceful and wise male personification of wisdom, Manjushri, or as more wrathful personifications of virtue, such as Vajrakilaya. Men do these practices in exactly the same manner. There are, in fact, endless such role models beyond the prison of conventional human gender roles available to Buddhist practitioners. Now, it's up to us to imitate the Buddhas and bodhisattvas in becoming free of the prison of gender roles.

COMMON MISTAKES REGARDING FREEDOM FROM THE PRISON OF GENDER ROLES

When people are first made aware that conventional gender roles are a prison, rather than just "the way things are," their first reaction is often denial that these gender roles are a problem at all. Denial is commonly the first reaction people have when hearing Buddhist teachings, especially teachings on the first and second Noble Truths. Denial of the first truth takes the form of claiming, "This isn't suffering. It's just the way things are." Gender roles are not a prison, because there is no alternative. That gender roles involve suffering is denied on the basis of purported traits shared by most or all members of each gender. These are often based in perceived biological certainties for each sex. Women are more suited to childcare because they give birth. The Western version of that thesis, popular when I was young, was Sigmund Freud's assertion "Anatomy is destiny." So we were given this advice: "Conform and adjust. That's the greatest level of happiness you can achieve." The Buddhist equivalent would be if our Buddhist teachers told us that there is no release from suffering, so grab what happiness you can in samsara, even though it will always be ultimately unsatisfactory.

A more subtle level of denial involves raising common stereotypes about men and women to the level of real truths about them, which then justifies conventional gender roles. Again, the argument goes that these roles can't be unfair or a prison, because they are accurate descriptions about women and men. One of the most common patriarchal justifications for male-dominant gender roles, used in Buddhism as well as more widely, is the claim that men are more rational whereas women are more emotional, so men need to control women and society. Isn't that obvious? One version of this thesis was the title of a best-selling book on relationships in the 1990s: *Men Are from Mars, Women Are from Venus*. The premise is that men and women are just different and there are no notable exceptions to these stereotypes.

A slightly different version of this thesis was frequently cited in early second-wave feminism. Numerous studies asked people to identify which in a long list of traits described the ideal man, the ideal woman, and the ideal human being. Most of the traits were paired opposites, such as active or passive, rational or emotional, and so on. In all cases, the traits that were said to describe the ideal male were also said to describe the ideal human, but none of the traits chosen to describe the ideal female were considered to be ideal for a human being. If ideal human traits are more commonly found in men than in women, obviously male-dominant gender roles are better for everyone. If people believe in these stereotypes and conform to them, clearly the result will be the mutual incompetence that is the final product of the prison of gender roles discussed at the end of chapter 3. But, on Buddhist grounds, these stereotypes, insofar as they are accurate, could only apply to "untaught, ignorant" people who had not yet done their homework of thoroughly studying the self and disowning what not really "theirs." Their relative accuracy confers on them no real existence. Only "untaught, ignorant" people believe that their thoughts need to be believed in.

Taking another perspective, using secular logic, conventional gender roles are justified on grounds of statistical averages. Many suppose such averages appear to be both fairer and more "scientific" than folk stereotypes about women's and men's "natures." Girls and boys do demonstrate different bell curves regarding relative abilities in quantitative versus verbal skills and so on. Thus, it is presumed to be reasonable, not prejudicial, to steer boys toward STEM careers. Isn't that realistic and fair? But what about girls who love and excel in math and sciences? Averages don't limit specific individuals in the same way that purported traits essential to each sex would. That is why they will not work as the basis for a "better" set of gender roles. Some individuals within the various gender groups may not find the roles toward which they are directed to be too oppressive, because they fit within the averages for their group. Their test scores give rise to those averages on which generalizations about recommended gender roles are based. But those who don't fit within the averages that characterize their gender will be oppressed by roles based on statistical averages. To recall a story about myself that I told in chapter 3, such logic was the justification used by the professor who claimed that I should not receive a prestigious graduate fellowship because I am a woman. More women than men graduate students did drop out without finishing their degrees at that time; therefore, according to him, my competence in and love of my chosen field should be irrelevant. In his logic, that professor omitted all the conditioned, non-ultimate, interdependent causes and conditions that encourage more women than men not to finish their degrees—most importantly, the rigid set of expectations placed on men and women. Changes in the conditioned interdependent matrix in which men and women are all immersed, such as greater mental flexibility on everyone's part, would easily and completely change that relative situation.

When people become aware that the conventional gender roles to which they have given allegiance are problematic in some ways, are unsatisfactory, and result in suffering, as allegiance to any conditioned phenomenon always does, they then suggest that the solution is a new set of "better," reformed, "fairer" set of gender roles. Usually the proposed new set of roles is presented as more "egalitarian." Some of the privileges of the more dominant sex are opened up to some extent to the other sex, without any prospect of either true equality or genuine freedom from a prison of gender roles—just a different prison. Such partial solutions are commonly offered to various groups who begin to protest their inferior status in the whole society. For example, women are offered more education, even equal educations, but after they leave school, they still find themselves trapped under a glass ceiling in their profession and they face more liabilities when becoming parents than do their male counterparts in the same profession. Or homosexuals in long-term partnerships who desire the economic and legal advantages available to their heterosexual counterparts who marry are offered "domestic partnerships" instead. But domestic partnerships don't offer all the legal protections afforded by marriage nor the same emotional and social comforts. Clearly, racial and cultural minorities routinely face the same situation of slightly improved but still inferior status within society as a whole. The problem with such "solutions" is that people to whom they are applied are still defined in terms of some relative identity—sex, gender, race, sexual orientation—that has been given a level of reality, true existence, or ultimacy that it simply does not possess. As it has often been put, this solution of widening the prison may put a few cracks in its walls, but it is still a prison with narrow limits, and few can get out through those small cracks.

A more sophisticated alternative to the patriarchal prison of gender roles, proposed by some feminists and sometimes also by Buddhists, is a dualistic gender essentialism of complementary qualities. This complementarity is more often a complementarity between "masculine" and "feminine" than between women and men. According to this view, desirable and necessary human qualities can validly be categorized as either "feminine" or "masculine," and the masculine and feminine qualities are of equal value. Then it is claimed that, by some mysterious process, both women and men are both "masculine" and "feminine"! This is a complex, multipart hypothesis that sometimes seems to address problems inherent in traditional gender roles.

The starting point for variants of these hypotheses is the insight that qualities associated with women in patriarchal systems have been unfairly and inaccurately denigrated. They are necessary to the overall functioning of the system. Without what women do, especially taking care of men and children, these systems would disintegrate. Because their work is necessary and useful, we should elevate it, dignify it, and even glorify it. It should be called "the feminine" and no longer limited to or expected of women alone. The "feminine" is claimed to be of equal value with the "masculine."

Such language is often extremely seductive to women immersed in patriarchal systems in which we have been consistently taught how unimportant and lowly we are compared to men. The value of our work has been denied. Prestige and privileges have not been available to us, nor have education and leadership roles. Is it any wonder that we develop low self-esteem? Such language about the dignity of the feminine is in stark contrast to most of the messages, especially religious messages, we have heard all our lives. The images of the feminine, both verbal and artistic, that emerge in religious contexts that encourage and allow such messages are profound and beautiful. They are so appealing and elevated. In systems in which we have been so denigrated, such a message makes us feel better about ourselves. No wonder many women respond eagerly!

But many wonder how these images of the feminine actually affect women and what changes for us "on the ground," as we say. It is clear that in many religious contexts, men are eager to take on symbolically the now-valued aspects of femininity. It is less clear whether they are any more willing to take on aspects of women's work that are mundane, repetitious, boring, and devalued. Even though the complementary "masculine" is supposed to be available to women as well, it is also unclear whether women can now frequently take roles usually held by men, such as being a Buddhist dharma teacher. Though the *idea* of gender complementarity in which masculine and feminine virtues are of equal value and equally available to both women and men is attractive, one must ask whether it has cut into male dominance in any way. Does it diminish the conditions that make female rebirth woeful? The answer to those questions inclines much more to the negative than the positive.

Systems of symbolic complementary dualisms between masculine and feminine are ubiquitous in world religions, so they must satisfy some deep psychological and religious need. There are many variants. Some systems, with examples in recent Western feminism, reverse patriarchal dualisms without introducing complementarity between men and women. As a result of the intense anger women experience over having been wounded so severely in patriarchy, now the qualities associated with women are elevated as important and good, while those associated with men are denigrated. Men's tendency to violence is contrasted negatively with the more peaceful tendencies supposedly more characteristic of women. For example, some people claim that if women ruled the world, warfare would be less common. These kinds of Western feminism must be what drives Asian stereotypes about feminism. But Western Buddhist feminists have not preached this version of feminism.

Historically, and in most contemporary examples, genuine symbolic complementarity is more common. But how do some things come to be labeled "feminine" or "masculine"? Is there any logic to the labels? Why, for example, in some Vajrayana Buddhist symbol systems of gender complementarity is femininity equated with wisdom and the masculinity with compassion? Some less-informed commentators try to prove gender essentialism by claiming cross-cultural uniformity for these symbolic associations. But that uniformity is simply not the case, as demonstrated by the fact that most people are surprised by the Vajrayana symbolism when they first hear of it. Another great danger to symbolic gender complementarity is the claim that women have more of the feminine qualities than men do, and vice versa. That would only be a prettier version of the prison of gender roles. How useful could it be for Vajrayana Buddhists to claim that women are wiser than men because in the wisdom-compassion complementarity, wisdom is feminine? Fortunately in the Buddhist case, because the teachings on egolessness and emptiness are so definitive, any possibility of gender essentialism is undercut. Furthermore, in Vajrayana Buddhist practice, one's specific physiological gender is irrelevant to how one does practices involving symbolism of gender complementarity. Additionally, from a Buddhist point of view, one must ask whether any system that is still dualistic could be fully adequate in the long run.

Why are systems of symbolic gender complementarity so appealing? I believe people find genuine psychological-spiritual comfort in seeing symbols of ultimacy that resemble themselves—as in my own story of the female angels and my grief when they were taken away from me. The contrast here is between Western monotheistic symbol systems, which are almost devoid of any female ultimates, and the rest of the world, which finds such male monotheism incomprehensible. As a veteran of the Goddess movement in Western feminist theology, I know what I am talking about. A religious symbol system in which the Ultimate is always only male, period, is incredibly depriving. In the Goddess movement, we once thought that having dignified feminine symbolism in the system would make all the difference. But in the long run, we had to notice that even religious symbol systems that included fully adequate symbolic gender complementarity in their theologies were still male-dominated socially, even if they provided some psychological compensation not present in male monotheisms.

This is the case even with Vajrayana Buddhist symbol systems of gender complementarity, which are as evenhanded and elevated as any I have encountered in my extensive study of such symbolisms. Nevertheless, on the ground in Tibetan society, women are still deprived and disadvantaged in many ways, to the extent that one of the Tibetan terms for "woman" literally means "born low." As Kim Gutschow says in her 2004 study, *Being a Buddhist Nun* (and as we saw in the previous chapter), despite these exalted feminine symbols that are of equal dignity with male symbols, "The bottom line is clear. No Buddhist in her right mind desires a female body."[21] These symbol systems can be a useful skillful means, especially psychologically, to help overcome certain negative effects of living in a prison of gender roles. I am not criticizing them on those grounds. But they are not a complete antidote to patriarchal social systems. Though women who are able to do these exalted practices involving symbolisms of gender complementarity do them exactly as do men, women are much less likely to be in a social position to be able to do such practices at all. We still have to do other work to break out of the prison of gender roles.

WHAT DOES FREEDOM FROM THE PRISON OF GENDER ROLES LOOK LIKE?

Proposed alternatives to the prison of gender roles that deny such roles are a prison and argue that they are simply accurate descriptions of men and women, that try to construct a better, fairer set of gender roles, or that try to elevate "femininity" into parity with "masculinity" will nonetheless still be a prison of gender roles for some. It will still be "the system" that I identified so early in my life as the real source of my frustration rather than my female body. It is not possible to free people from the prison of gender roles by proposing a different grand plan that should work for everyone, which has been the kind of solution most often proposed to date. That solution simply will not work. As with issues of religious diversity, people are simply too distinctive for one "system" to be universally appropriate or applicable.

If we do not propose a different grand plan that will finally work for everyone, what is the solution? We could simply admit there is no one grand solution. There will not be much uniformity about what people do with their sexed bodies in a society free of the prison of gender roles. All the relevant ethical options for utilizing the "precious human birth" that Buddhists love to talk about will be available to all, whatever their sexed bodies may look like, whether or not those bodies were born with their current sexual equipment. What else could it possibly mean to talk about enlightened mind beyond gender, neither male nor female? If every sexed body is forced into the gender role deemed appropriate for it, how could anyone ever break free to a state of mind that is no longer obsessed with gender roles and no longer clings to them, either to their own perceived roles or those of others. It's quite simple. If we give up clinging to gender identity, there is no longer anything inside or outside of oneself that compels someone to be or feel a certain way because of the shape of their bodies. This would be

quite different from "the system" that led me to locate my frustrations in my female body when I was a girl.[22]

It should take only a moment's reflection to realize that if the
problem is *clinging* to the conventional given set of gender roles,
the solution cannot be *imposing* a different, "new and improved"
set of gender roles. That would simply be *clinging* to a different set
of conventions. For Buddhists, clinging is always what causes suffering. Thus, while different visionaries may have different worthy
ideas about better ways to organize society and male-female relationships, we all need to remember not to absolutize our relative
solutions and suggestions. Feminists are just as guilty of forgetting
this requirement as anyone else. Clinging to a feminist set of ideas
about gender is just as much subverting enlightenment through
clinging to a prison of gender roles as clinging to any other set of
gender roles would be.

It's not the content of any gender roles that is all that bad. Neither "men's work" nor "women's work" is inherently dehumanizing or to be avoided. The dehumanizing happens when the specific
task is linked with either men or women. Cooking can be skilled
and interesting and it has to be done. I enjoy it sometimes. But I
would resent being required to do it three times a day every day
of the year for the men and children I'm supposed to take care of,
just because I have a female body. Nor would I want to be forced
to enter military service if I had a male body, nor prohibited from
it because I am a woman. As an adult, I willingly dust my many
beautiful antique lamps, even though I dreaded being condemned
to a life of "dusting lamps" when I was a girl. To cite another pertinent example, I now type quite well, but when I was a young
woman I made sure that I didn't type too well; otherwise I would
have been forced into a secretarial role. But now that computers
are so omnipresent, men have to be able to type as well.

I've spend my entire life in a "male" field, a field so "male" that
when I entered it, more women had PhDs in physics than in religious studies. (Physics was then labeled a "male field.") When I
entered the Divinity School at the University of Chicago, twelve
of the four hundred students were women and the professors were

horrified. "What are we going to do with all those women who now want to study religion?" they asked. Some of them changed the content of their lectures because of the presence of women in the classroom. This "male" field suits me perfectly. It and my female body get along quite well. The "male" role of dharma teaching suits me even better. Am I more male or female? Who knows? Who cares? I've often been told I'm too masculine for a woman, which usually means I'm too confident, competent, and successful. Or that I have a male mind and a female body! That comment strikes me as quite ridiculous. My vagina marks my body as female, but how can a mind be either male or female? It seems increasingly ridiculous to label anything except penises or vaginas male or female, or to assume anything about what goes with either of them.

All these examples demonstrate the difference between being gendered, being male or female, and the prison of gender roles. Being gendered does not subvert enlightenment, but *clinging* to gender identity does. Such a conclusion should not surprise anyone with modest Buddhist knowledge. The second of the Noble Truths tells us that clinging is the cause of our suffering. How could it be different when we are fixated on what the shape of our bodies *must mean* or how it must limit us, or when we cling to gender identity so strongly that we are willing to limit what others with differently shaped bodies can do in the name of dharma? Our clinging to our notions of gender can cause us suffering, but it can also cause others to suffer—something that should bother any Buddhist committed to Buddhist ethics.

Whenever I have proposed such freedom from the prison of gender roles and someone argues in response, "But men and women are different! That has to mean something! There have to be limits!" usually that argument is coming from a man trying to preserve some arena of male privilege. Men and women are different! What does that mean? Women and women, men and men, are also different! That all women are not the same as all other women nor all men the same as all other men is never taken into account by those arguing that there have to be definite gender roles. For myself, I accept that biologically I am a woman, a fact that is readily obvious to others. But as I've already said—that doesn't give you much reliable information about me. So stop projecting your version of the prison of gender role onto me. Recognize, as the Buddha taught, that such thoughts are not really "you" or "yours," so stop identifying with them, stop solidifying them, as many would say in colloquial English dharma-speak. Therefore, abandoning them would be for "welfare and happiness" of both self and other.

Some will ask, "But isn't there something we can prescribe, some rules we can insist upon?" I would answer that question in the affirmative. The relevant question to ask of any option or set of practices that people put together is whether or not it promotes everyone's ability to recognize that natural state of mind beyond gender, that state of mind not bound by relative references. Practices, whether social or individual, that do not should be abandoned. There may be some guidelines about that, but they do not involve gender roles specific to biological males and females. Discipline and deep contemplation will be necessary. Renunciation of many things valued in the conventional world of "ordinary worldlings" will be necessary. But dividing people into groups based on biological sex has never proved to promote discipline, contemplation, and renunciation for both biological women and men. Nor does dividing people into groups, some of which are defined as servants of other groups, whose only role is to take care of them, work well to promote recognition of the natural, enlightened state of mind beyond gender. If Buddhists want to be serious about the purported enlightened state of mind, beyond gender, neither male nor female, then I suggest we have to stop advocating any version of the prison of gender roles.

But, I suspect, some will still be uncomfortable and want more precise, detailed rules governing gender-specific behavior and interactions between women and men. How will people know how to behave if they don't have clear rules? Won't we have too much disorder if we don't have precise, specific rules? But how to prevent a set of rules specific for each sex and their interactions from degenerating into a prison of gender roles? It seems to me that would be a difficult, if not impossible, task. Additionally, I would suggest that we Buddhists already have all the guidelines we need, in the form of the Eightfold Path and the basic precepts. In them, the guidelines are exactly the same for each gender. Don't harm. Don't misuse sexuality, using it in ways that harm self or other. What more do we need?

Predictably, whenever someone suggests that it would be good dharma practice to stop promoting any version of the prison of gender roles, someone will complain that such a proposal "genderizes the dharma" and makes a big deal out of gender. It leaves me shaking my head in incredulity. How can making gender *less* determinative in Buddhist life and institutions be "genderizing the dharma"? I would have thought that relying on gender to determine, for example, which people, women or men, can become monastics, would be "genderizing the dharma." Or I would have thought that practices such as giving even the most junior monk precedence over the most senior nun is genderizing the dharma. Such practices make an irrelevant factor, one's sex, the criterion for taking on roles and practices that are valued in Buddhism while at the same time ignoring much more relevant factors, such as seniority or fitness for the monastic lifestyle. Isn't that making a "big deal" out of gender?

Yet I cannot tell you how often I have been accused of "genderizing the dharma" for doing nothing more than pointing out how genderized dharma already is! One can only reply that dharma became genderized when one's sex became a determining factor in what one could or couldn't do in terms of dharma practice. Those of us who point out such things had nothing to do with "genderizing the dharma"! In fact, if the suggestions we put forward were taken seriously, dharma would be far less gendered. The way to stop genderizing the dharma and to stop making a big deal out of gender is to stop treating men and women so differently! That so many, even prominent, well-known teachers with a great deal of authority, have such difficulty grasping this simple point demonstrates how unreflective and conventional they have become. In terms of studying the self and accomplishing the way of enlightenment, it is crucial to remember that samsaric ego binds us by convincing us that what we do habitually is truly "ours" and can be trusted. The Buddha's advice quoted at the beginning of this chapter (page 72) should be recalled again.

I find it touching that many commentators worry that women who point out how genderized dharma already is and would like dharma to be less genderized have "an ego problem" and that, therefore, our dharmic well-being is in serious jeopardy. Their solution is that we should not object to the prison of gender roles that is already in place and we should just pay more attention to our dharma practice. After all, we are reminded again, enlightened mind is beyond gender, neither male nor female. But since when is it more dharmic, more demonstrative of some realization, to acquiesce mindlessly to an inappropriate status quo than it is to use the *prajna*, the finely honed, detached intellect, that practice brings, to improve the dharmic situation for everyone, male as well as female? Perhaps the clarity with which we see that the prison of gender roles is dharmically inappropriate is evidence that we have some acquaintance with that nongendered awakened state of mind! Because we have taken bodhisattva vows and wish to help others, we wish to dismantle practices that obviously are of no help to anyone, female or male, who wishes to study the self and attain the way of enlightenment. It would be impossible to demonstrate that gender hierarchies in any way help male practitioners study the self and attain the way of enlightenment, but it is quite easy to demonstrate that they actually hinder women greatly.

I find it amusing that the same commentators who worry about women damaging their dharma practice by not acquiescing to the status quo have no similar worries about men who argue vociferously to retain their gender privilege. If women who don't accept a status quo have "an ego problem," why don't men who defend and argue in favor of that same status quo also have an ego problem? One would think, given that the status quo advantages them, men would be in greater danger of lapsing into egoistic self-grasping, especially when they both demean women who advocate a less genderized dharma and also strongly advocate maintaining the status quo of their gender privilege!

As a concrete example, I once heard a story about a female student who asked a female teacher if it was true that a senior nun had to bow down to even a baby monk. The teacher replied that if a woman experienced difficulty bowing to a male baby, she definitely had an ego problem. No problems so far, and this student may have needed a bit of a dharmic slap from a teacher. But problems remain. Why aren't men expected to bow to girls under similar circumstances? Are there even any similar reverse circumstances? The double standard is the problem, not asking women to bow to men when appropriate. Any woman who couldn't is definitely out of line.

Buddhists defending the status quo often cite "karma" as the reason why no one should object to current conditions or try to improve that situation in the future. Teachings on karma are at the heart of the Buddhist understanding of the world and would be considered to be nonnegotiable by all teachers. One cannot deny that there is karma and still be Buddhist. Karma, "dependent arising," is a difficult topic, often seriously misunderstood and misused. The most prevalent misunderstanding is that "karma" involves unalterable fate to which one is subject, about which nothing can be done. Teachings on karma are sometimes said to be about cause and effect, but when I teach about dependent arising, I often suggest that it is much more appropriate to think of karma as being about "effect and cause." The subtle difference is important. Any present situation is as it is; it is an effect and obviously cannot be altered. But what one does with this present situation is *not* pre-determined. What one does with the present is the cause that helps determine future outcomes. The key point in Buddhist discipline is to work wisely and proactively with present circumstance so that present difficulties are alleviated in the future. Because we Buddhists have inherited a situation of male-dominated institutions does not mean that is the way things should be or that things should stay that way.

While individuals can take personal comfort in teachings about karma when confronting difficult circumstances, and they can take responsibility for their part in bringing about the present situation, such teachings are easily misused, especially when directed at others to justify their present suffering—as in saying, "It's your karma to be poor, to be abused, to be subjected to male dominance, so just submit to it." It is common to misuse teachings about karma in this way to discourage people who live in difficult circumstances from trying to change their situations, claiming instead that they should just accept their situations because they are appropriate and are something they "created" themselves. Certainly teachings on karma have been used in this way to reconcile women to male dominance by claiming that to be born female in a male-dominated system is the result of "karma." So rather than trying to change the system, one should submit to it, hoping to be reborn as a male in a future life.

Thus privilege is claimed to be the result of karma and, as such, appropriate, even justified. But privilege involves a hierarchy in which others are less well off in some way. Some are "up," while others are "down." Often the "up" status of some is directly dependent on the "down" status of others. Traditional Buddhist thought usually finds that situation unproblematic. So, in fact, does much non-Buddhist thought. In many situations of interdependent hierarchies, for some to have privilege, others must be underprivileged. But those who are "on top" feel strongly that they have "earned" their privileged status and "deserve" it. Such claims are especially strong regarding wealth and privilege hierarchies. Even more problematic, people who inherit advantageous circumstances sometimes even fail to recognize that they are privileged. But one could also think quite differently about this dynamic. If one uses one's privileged status to oppress others, would that not create "negative karma" for oneself, using traditional ways of talking about and understanding karma? So if one is on the "up" side of a hierarchy, what does that mean about how one should behave?

Among some social critics, including many feminists, hierarchy is regarded negatively. However, some hierarchy is required in Buddhism. Liberating Buddhist teachings are subtle and cannot be subjected to acceptance by popular acclaim. Several times already, we have been reminded that the historical Buddha hesitated to teach what he had understood during his enlightenment experience because it is not what most people want to hear. Therefore, teachers cannot be elected and there must be a hierarchy between those who understand the teachings more well and less well. That kind of hierarchy is not a problem. The problem is arbitrary hierarchies, those based on criteria irrelevant to the task at hand. Obviously, in terms of the issues being discussed, men have absolutely no real advantage over women when it comes to being able to understand the dharma and teach it well. However, throughout Buddhist history, men have monopolized roles of dharma teaching. Recognition as a teacher is not necessarily the same thing as deep realization of the awakened state of mind. Probably there have been many unrecognized, unacknowledged teachers throughout Buddhist history. But that situation is to no one's benefit. Thus, from my earliest days as a dharma student, I have insisted that the acid test of whether Buddhism has transcended its historical male dominance for something more appropriate is whether or not approximately half the dharma teachers are women.

In some Buddhist circles, any critical inquiry into current events is discouraged. Students are made to feel guilty about their interest in things such as engaged-Buddhist movements. It is claimed that such concerns cannot help anyway but instead compromise one's meditation practice. One of the arguments is that because social problems are intractable, they cannot be solved, leading to frustration, depression, and anger, all attitudes at odds with the enlightened mind. Alternatively, it is argued, one cannot avoid developing attachment if one tries to promote social reform or any kind of social betterment. And attachment, aka "clinging," is even more problematic than anger or depression for one seeking the way of enlightenment. So better just to focus on one's own practice. These warnings have genuine validity. Students still in training who also become involved in one "cause" or another often do develop all the tendencies listed above. They easily fall prey to emotionalism. In the West, language of justice and rights, terms not easily found in more traditional Buddhism, is common and has often been influential in the earlier formation of those newer to Buddhist practice. Such students often develop strong ideologies about their causes and become quite opinionated.

For a dharma teacher, such students can be challenging to work with. Opinionatedness and ideology are discouraged in meditation students for the practical reason that they solve nothing and only make the situation worse for both the student herself and those about whom she is concerned. It is difficult to watch someone be in as much pain as the newer student still entangled in overly emotional concern with some cause. Yet there is also a lot of good heart and some wisdom in the student's passionate involvement in her cause. What will the outcome be? Some teachers recommend, even insist, that the student renounce her concern for anything other than dharma and, perhaps, her own everyday life. Great skill on the teacher's part is required at this point. In trying to tame the student's ideology, one does not want to veer into promoting apathy, which is also not appropriate dharmic advice. Outsiders to Buddhism often think that Buddhism must promote apathy, given how much emphasis there is on the problems with attachment and the virtues of detachment. But apathy easily falls into the category of one of the "poisons of emptiness," mistakes often made by students who have some insight into emptiness. This mistake often takes the form of saying something like "Because everything is empty, nothing matters, so I can do whatever I want or not take responsible action."[23] One must be careful not to promote the incorrect assumption that the only alternatives are either ideological, angry entanglement in a cause or withdrawal from involvement into apathy or indifference.

Practice, however, provides a middle path between angry ideology and apathetic withdrawal. This is one of the most useful contributions Buddhist disciplines can make to contemporary discussions. The language of "self-righteous anger" is deeply entrenched in Western discourse on social issues, and many otherwise competent and wise thinkers remain plagued by it for many years, in some cases even after they have acquaintance with Buddhist thought and practice. Often they still fear that the only alternative is apathy. They still fear dualism—if I'm not this, I'll be that. Unless I'm angry, I won't care at all.

From the other side, some Buddhists find it difficult to recognize, especially when they disagree with someone about a controversial issue, that it is possible to hold a viewpoint and yet not be angry and ideological, that a viewpoint can be held with equanimity. Penetrating insight undoes both apathy and attachment with one blow of Manjushri's sword. This should not be surprising. Enlightened mind beyond gender is not a blank state of mind. It is intelligent but without ideology. Because it recognizes that its verbalizations of insight can never be fully adequate, it holds them lightly. Therefore it is completely flexible. The verbalization of insight will change without struggle when further information and better reasoning make such change appropriate. But it is also fearless and fully able to withstand attack and confrontation with equanimity, and to stand its own ground without resort to aggression.

I have discovered this dynamic many times in my presentations of Buddhist feminism. Sometimes others insist that my only motivation for not supporting male dominance must be that I am angry. But those days are long over. What I have often found is that those who dislike my feminism think I should automatically defer to them, I suppose because they are so used to having women defer to them. When I don't defer, they themselves become extremely angry.

In one notable encounter, a man demanded in an aggressive and authoritative manner that I give in to his position, which was that generic masculine language in Buddhist liturgies was not a problem. He was not at all willing to discuss the issues I was bringing up rationally. Instead, he did his best to egg me into an angry response to him. Then he would be justified in simply rejecting me and my position: "See! I told you she's just an angry feminist bitch!" But I didn't take the bait in any way, demonstrating both steadfastness and equanimity. Eventually, he caved and said that he wanted to discuss the points I was making. After several hours of discussion he conceded, "You're right!" The next day he announced to those assembled for a large dharma program that if they preferred to change the language of an important text from generic masculine to gender-inclusive and neutral language, that was acceptable.

Would it not have been so much simpler to discuss the issues from the beginning, instead of asserting male privilege and dominance? It takes a good bit of training neither to become angry, thus losing the discussion by default, nor to simply give in because that's what women are trained to do when men assert male dominance. Need I report that this confrontation involved a male Buddhist teacher whose position in the teaching hierarchy was higher than mine? I tell this story to demonstrate that insight paired with equanimity can be effective, far more effective than simply resorting to anger when faced with aggression. I also tell this story to illustrate that giving up on anger as the fuel that maintains one's sense of urgency about something that needs to be changed does not mean that one becomes apathetic and just gives in to convention and the status quo.

So, in the final analysis, what does freedom from the prison of gender roles look like? It has nothing to do with whether one is a man or a woman, or even whether one lives a more traditional or a more radical lifestyle. It has everything to do with one's state of mind. Is it starting to approach that enlightened state of mind beyond gender? If so, it will not be characterized by anger and will not strongly hold any ideology. One's mind will be utterly flexible and will dwell easily in equanimity, but it will not confuse equanimity and apathy. The mind state of someone who insists that male dominance and the prison of gender roles in any of its forms are unproblematic doesn't qualify. She or he still holds an ideology. Nor would holding a "feminist" position necessarily mean that one is approaching that freer state of mind. It depends on the flexibility and ease of his or her state of mind. Whatever one comes up with, one holds that position and that identity lightly. Its relative character is clearly recognized. It is not made into an ultimate. If one has truly studied the self, then one can forget it, and relax.

FIVE

INDIGENOUS BUDDHIST FEMINISM

Asian Buddhists, as well as Western Buddhists, frequently claim that "feminism" is a "Western" innovation and, therefore, not relevant to Buddhists. This claim always leaves me incredulous. For one thing, one cannot prove that something is irrelevant to Buddhism or Buddhists by citing its Western origins. Many of the Asian Buddhists I know would be extremely reluctant to give up their cell phones and many other technologies, despite their Western origins. But there is a much more basic reason why this claim leaves me incredulous. Granted, "feminism" is a Western term, but what it means and encompasses is not only compatible with Buddhism but is already deeply embedded in many Buddhist texts from virtually all periods of Buddhist history and all schools of Buddhism. From the beginnings of Buddhism throughout its history, some Buddhists have always made fun of and rejected Buddhism's more male-dominant strata. To claim that feminism is irrelevant to Buddhism, Buddhists would have to ignore many definitive texts that represent important teachers, from the historical Buddha to Padmasambhava, making claims that, were a Western Buddhist feminist to make an identical claim, would immediately be rejected by some because of its alleged Western "feminism." In recent years, I have begun to focus on what I call "indigenous Buddhist feminism" by demonstrating how prevalent these "feminist" texts, which could not possibly derive from Western influences, actually are. I am not trying to persuade Buddhists to imitate Western practices and Western values.

In their justifiable attempts to avoid inappropriate Western colonial initiatives, why would Buddhists ignore one of the Buddhist tradition's most precious insights—that gender is ultimately unreal and irrelevant. As I have repeatedly demonstrated in previous chapters, the West cannot claim any superiority in its gender practices until recently, if even then. I am urging Buddhists to live up to the potential and vision of our own tradition regarding gender equality and equity, to promote social practices that enable women and men equally to reach that enlightened state of mind beyond gender—neither male nor female—to quote the slogan that so many Buddhists love. To do that, Buddhists will have to ignore many other dimensions of traditional Buddhism, especially many institutional practices that point in the opposite direction and involve significant male privilege. As I have written many times, the view that promotes gender neutrality and equality and that praises the enlightened mind beyond gender is incompatible with institutional practices of male dominance. Those male-dominant practices may have been unavoidable before modern medicine changed required gender roles so much, but nothing is worse than hanging on to outmoded, irrelevant practices simply because they are familiar. With our facility at penetrating analysis, Buddhists should easily be able to penetrate and resolve this incompatibility between view and practice.

Of course, to make these claims about feminism being indigenous to Buddhism, we have to be clear about what is meant by "feminism." Herein, I fear, lies much of the problem. Even in the West (especially in the West?), feminism is routinely trivialized and misrepresented in popular media. The only relevant definitions of feminism in this context are my consistently used definition—freedom from the prison of gender roles—and a less personal definition, based on the understanding that women and men are equally human and thus equally entitled to what can make a human birth "precious" in Buddhist understandings of the great good fortune that can accompany a human rebirth. What makes a human birth worthwhile is the possibility of finding that enlightened state of mind beyond gender, neither male nor female, which the prison of gender roles subverts. Feminism, properly understood, is not about female supremacy or about hating men. We feminists are not positively disposed toward male privilege and dominance, but disliking such evil social practices has nothing to do with hating men. It is sad when people refuse to see the distinction between these two things, claiming that feminists must be women who were "unlucky in love" or dislike men. Of course, in patriarchal or male-dominated social situations, applying "feminist" reforms would result in improved situations for women and girls over their status quo. How could that possibly be a problem for anyone?

THE POLITICS OF SCHOLARSHIP

Buddhist studies scholarship, whether Asian or Western, is not an objective practice in which everyone comes up with the same results concerning questions such as which texts are important and how they should be interpreted. Sometimes some texts are selected to receive far more attention than is warranted, and sometimes relevant texts are ignored for centuries or by certain groups of interpreters. Both processes have deeply affected how texts pertaining to indigenous Buddhist feminism have been received both by Buddhists and by Western scholars of Buddhism. Many texts seem to have received less attention from Buddhists than they deserve. For example, texts discussed in chapter 4 on Buddhist perceptions of humanity as genuinely two-sexed, which are so different from Western texts about the priority of the male and the derived character of the female, have been underutilized by Buddhists. They so clearly undercut Buddhist male-dominant institutions, which are more in accord with Western male-dominated religious institutions than with the Buddhist understanding that humanity is genuinely two-sexed.

At least for Western Buddhists, however, androcentrism on the part of Western Buddhist studies scholars has seriously skewed how texts are selected for inclusion in textbooks on Buddhism and which elements of the Buddhist heritage are emphasized in such books. Needless to say, such interpretive practices would seriously affect what Western Buddhists know about their tradition. Androcentrism is different from male dominance, and that distinction is important. Male dominance, aka patriarchy, is a way of organizing society so that men control a society and its institutions. In a patriarchal society, women may be largely invisible to outside observers, including scholars, and may seem to them to be uninteresting or unimportant, to the extent that women don't receive inclusion in descriptions of that society or religion—which is androcentrism. Such was the status of the field of religious studies when I entered it as a graduate student in the mid-1960s. I was seriously discouraged from studying women's religious lives and roles because androcentric Western scholars had "determined" that women had no religious lives of note, that it was waste of scholarly energy to even look into them. I countered that even in male-dominated religions, women had religious lives, roles, and opinions. In my earliest research I found that androcentric scholars, predisposed to think that women are uninteresting and unimportant, had overlooked a great deal of relevant data regarding the religion they were studying.[1] Women's studies scholarship discovered the same dynamic over and over again. It is important to understand that androcentrism is a set of presuppositions *residing in the scholars' minds*, not something *out there* in the data being studied and observed by scholars. It is equally important to realize that the Western academy in general was not only male dominated but was also completely androcentric until relatively recently, and it still is in many cases. Western Buddhist studies is no exception to this generalization.

Such androcentric scholars seem, in addition, to exaggerate and delight in the male dominance they "report." One small example still stands out in my mind many years later and still irritates me. During second-year Sanskrit, which I studied during the 1967–1968 school year, for some reason the term "yogi," a practitioner of yoga, came up. The professor, eagerly and with a smirk and undue delight, explained that the feminine of that term would be "yogini." But, he proclaimed, actually there are no yoginis because the feminine of that term actually means "a witch." Not only was his delight in his conclusion irritating; he was wrong. I could not correct him at that time because I didn't yet have the appropriate knowledge. Anyone who knows anything about Vajrayana Buddhism is aware that the term "yogini" is frequently used positively for female practitioners; they are not assumed to be witches but are honored for their accomplishments. It should not take much imagination to appreciate how alienating this false information could be to a young female scholar already fighting for a toehold in an extremely male-dominated field. And yet male scholars insist that the playing field is completely level and that the working conditions faced by women scholars are exactly the same as those under which men work.

Western scholarly androcentrism significantly affects how scholars select texts or elements within texts to highlight, often giving them far more centrality than a less androcentric reading would give them. One example I have begun to emphasize in recent teachings involves the *Mahaparinibbana Sutta*, which has become one of my favorite texts to teach, especially to Mahayana and Vajrayana audiences, who usually do not know Pali Buddhist literature well. This is the longest *sutta* in the Pali Canon and narrates the last three months of the Buddha's life. There are many episodes in the text. I focus on several that make points that are relevant to a discussion of indigenous Buddhist feminism.

One of the more important episodes concerns the Buddha's decision to relinquish his life force, leading to his death three months later. In the stories found in the Pali suttas, Mara continues to challenge the Buddha throughout his life, unlike the narratives familiar to most people today, in which Mara's encounters with the Buddha end after the Buddha's enlightenment experience. In the third episode of the *Mahaparinibbana Sutta*, Mara again approaches the Buddha, telling him that it is time for him to attain *parinibbana*. His argument is that he, Mara, had made a similar suggestion to the Buddha immediately after his enlightenment, arguing with him at that time that there was no reason for the Buddha to continue living now that he had attained final release. But, at that time, the Buddha had rejected Mara's proposal on the grounds that he still had work to do but would attain parinibbana when that work had been completed. Mara argues that the Buddha has now completed the tasks he had set for himself, so he should enter parinibbana. The Buddha agrees and says that in three months, he will indeed attain parinibbana.

The conditions that needed to be fulfilled before the Buddha would declare that his work was completed are relevant. The Buddha had declared:

> I will not take final Nibbana till I have monks and disciples who are accomplished, trained, skilled, learned, knowers of the Dhamma, trained in conformity with the Dhamma, correctly trained and walking in the path of the Dhamma, who will pass on what they have gained from their Teacher, teach it, declare it, establish it, expound it, analyse it, make it clear. . . .[2]

In the repetitive style so characteristic of Pali texts and so annoying to modern readers, exactly the same conditions are laid out again, this time pertaining to "nuns and female disciples" and then twice more, pertaining to "laymen-followers" and finally to "laywomen-followers."[3] Both the Buddha and Mara agree that those conditions have been filled, whereupon the Buddha assures Mara that he will take parinibbana in three months.

This passage is noteworthy for the way it emphasizes that the Buddha's work is not complete until the sangha includes fully accomplished nuns, laymen, and laywomen. His work is not complete merely when there are only fully accomplished monks. This condition constitutes a severe reprimand to most contemporary Buddhist communities, which emphasize and support only monks while ignoring nuns and not even imagining that laypeople could take on serious roles as teachers and fully accomplished disciples. In this sutta, laywomen and laymen are not called upon merely to earn merit by giving monastics economic support. For the Buddha's mission to be complete, his community also requires fully accomplished laywomen and laymen followers. Among monastics, it is not sufficient that there be competent monks. Competent nuns are equally important. This passage is one of many Pali texts that emphasize that a complete Buddhist community must include the "fourfold sangha"—monks, nuns, laymen, and laywomen—not omitting nuns, as is so frequently done by contemporary forms of Buddhism. These passages are frequently overlooked both by Western scholars and by Buddhists arguing about restoring bhikshuni ordination.

In their anthologies of Buddhist texts and discussions of early Buddhism, Western scholars are more likely to focus on a different story: the story of how the historical Buddha was supposedly unwilling to allow women to renounce their conventional domestic lives for the monastic lifestyle. They seem to like that story a great deal, especially the coda in which the Buddha imposes eight highly discriminatory rules on nuns and claims that the dharma will only last half as long as it would have, had women not been allowed to become nuns. These scholars ignore at least three important points in focusing on this particular text, especially when they emphasize it to the exclusion of texts such as the *Mahaparinibbana Sutta* that emphasize the importance of the fourfold sangha.

First, the view that a proper sangha must include all four orders is more normative than a single text in which it appears that the nuns' order was something of an afterthought, if only because the assumption of the fourfold sangha is omnipresent in the early texts. Second, many contemporary textual scholars have concluded that the story of the Buddha's reluctance to incorporate the nuns' sangha into his community must be a later interpolation into the texts. It contradicts too much about the presence of the nuns' sangha that is commonplace in early Buddhist literature. Third, even if one wants to take the story of the Buddha's reluctance to ordain nuns at face value, it includes something highly indicative of early indigenous Buddhist feminism, something I pointed out in *Buddhism after Patriarchy*. In the story that patriarchal interpreters of Buddhism love to cite, the Buddha *changes his mind*. As the story is usually told, the Buddha seems firm in his decision to exclude women from the monastic sangha, having already refused his aunt's request three times, even after she took the desperate step of cutting her hair, putting on yellow rags, and following the Buddha barefoot to a distant location to which he had moved. Ananda then takes up the women's cause, asking the Buddha if women would be capable of attaining arhatship if they could take up the monastic lifestyle, to which the Buddha replies positively. With no more reasons to refuse the women's request, the Buddha gives in, though the eight heavy rules and the prediction of the swifter decline of the Buddha's teaching follow immediately in the text.[4] Why ignore the segment of the story that portrays the Buddha as changing his mind while emphasizing every other element of the story? That element of the story does indicate indigenous Buddhist feminism. Someone did not hesitate to include in this text a motif of the all-revered Buddha changing his mind about something important to women and much more positive for them than his earlier position. As I wrote in *Buddhism after Patriarchy*, if even the Buddha can change his mind about established Buddhist male dominance, so can any contemporary Buddhist patriarch. They have the role model they need.[5] I have often pointed out this motif in talks titled "How Clinging to Gender Identity Subverts Enlightenment," to the great displeasure of some in the audience. On one occasion, someone shouted, "No, he didn't change his mind!" What else could you possibly call it?

Many Buddhists who are reluctant to reinstate or establish bhikshuni ordination simply ignore how normative the fourfold sangha was to the historical Buddha. They make no mention of texts such as the *Mahaparinibbana Sutta* and its emphasis on the fourfold sangha in their arguments. Instead, they focus on legalities. The Buddha did not establish procedures for starting a bhikshuni sangha in a situation in which there is no current bhikshuni sangha. Monastic rule requires that nuns be ordained by a dual sangha of both nuns and monks, which is lacking in both the Theravada and Tibetan contexts. "So what are we to do?" they argue. "It's not that we're anti-women. We are just trying to follow the Buddha faithfully"—the same Buddha who emphasized that his work was not complete until his sangha included fully competent nuns and laywomen, as well as laymen. What's wrong with the Chinese nuns' sangha? They follow a different monastic law code. Or, in the weaker argument put forward by some, the Chinese are Mahayanists—which is irrelevant in this case, because there is no specifically Mahayana monastic law code. Or they will argue that one does not need monastic status to practice Buddhist disciplines and attain release, so it doesn't matter that women can't become nuns. That argument is certainly correct, but such monks never reverse the argument by applying it to themselves. If women don't need a monastic sangha to follow the Buddha's teachings, why do they? What justifies their privileged position, other than their male anatomy? As was argued about another matter, what's sauce for the goose is sauce for the gander. If women don't need the monastic sangha, neither do men. I have suggested to some of these *vinaya* scholars that in the long run, ethics must trump legalisms when there is a conflict between a legal precedent and an ethical norm, especially an ethical norm central to the religious tradition. Surely it is of ethical urgency to set up social conditions in which the clear preferences of the Buddha about nuns can become normative again, and in which women are not disadvantaged in seeking that enlightened state of mind beyond gender, neither male nor female, that Buddhists refer to so frequently when trying to discount feminist frustration with male dominance. How can a tradition that emphasizes compassion as much as does Buddhism allow uncompassionate legalisms to prevail over the compassionate intentions of its founders? To date, I have not received replies from those to whom I have made these arguments. But in any case, as I've noted many times, if it were the men's monastic ordination lineages that were at stake, I'm sure they'd figure it all out quickly and easily. They have in the past, both in Theravada and in Tibetan cases.[6]

One final example of the politics of scholarship is the notorious example of how androcentric Western scholars love to select texts that make Buddhism seem even more male dominant and misogynist than it actually is. There is a short passage near the end of the *Mahaparinibbana Sutta* that is often pulled out of this long text to be included in an anthology of Buddhist texts. But nothing is mentioned about the text as a whole or its emphasis on the fourfold sangha. The three months during which the Buddha had promised to live are over; the Buddha is ill and near death. In fact, he and the monks traveling with him have reached Kushinagar, his death place, and he is already lying between the two *sal* trees where he died. Interspersed between the Buddha's instructions on making pilgrimage to the places where the four main events of his life occurred and on how to deal with his body after his death, Ananda, who had interceded to persuade the Buddha to ordain women, is represented as asking a question:

> "Lord, how should we act towards women?" to which he replies, "Do not see them, Ananda." "But if we see them, how should we behave, Lord?" "Do not speak to them, Ananda." "But if they should speak to us, Lord, how should we behave?" "Practice mindfulness, Ananda."[7]

In verbal presentations of this text, with the proper setup I have had audiences hooting because this interpolation into the text at this point is so preposterous. Why would an editor choose this insertion into the text at this point? The Buddha and his disciples have had forty-five years to discuss how to conduct themselves with regard to women, but now, moments before his death is the proper time to bring up that topic! To say nothing of the fact that a few lines further on in the text, the Buddha praises Ananda for having been a good attendant who always knew the proper time to let not only monks but also nuns and laywomen have audiences with the Buddha. The editor's judgment is surely something about which one can speculate. But what about the judgment of numerous Western Buddhist studies scholars who have picked only these six lines out of a long text for inclusion in their anthologies, which are intended mainly for student audiences and others less knowledgeable about Buddhism?[8] As I have tried to demonstrate, such androcentrism resides in the minds of such scholars, from where they impose it on the Buddhist materials they claim to be studying.

CHANGING STORIES ABOUT THE WOMEN AROUND THE BUDDHA

The case for indigenous Buddhist feminism that predates Western feminism by centuries is strengthened by stories told about the women closest to the earthly Buddha in later literary traditions. In the most often recounted stories about the Buddha, we hear almost nothing about the most important women in his life, especially his foster mother, Pajapati, and his wife, Yasodhara. They are not portrayed as central characters in the earliest accounts of the life of the Buddha. In fact, in Bhikkhu Nanamoli's account of the Buddha's life story as narrated in Pali Canon texts, his wife doesn't even appear and Mahapajapati makes only a few cursory appearances.[9] In those early accounts, his (male) disciples are much more important to the narrative than the women with whom he was associated before his renunciation. Even the well-known story of how Siddhartha abandoned his wife and newborn son to pursue his own ends is not found in canonical accounts of his life. I think it is important for Buddhists to know that the "Sunday school" versions of the Buddha's life story known to almost every Buddhist are not the stories early Buddhists chose to tell about him.

In later Buddhist literature, from perhaps the second century C.E. to almost the present day, their stories were considerably expanded, demonstrating, among other things, the considerable freedom Buddhists felt to reinvent and modify their stories well into the development of Buddhism. Given this traditional flexibility, one wonders why there is reluctance to introduce new materials on the part of modern Buddhists, whether Asians or Westerners. Furthermore, the kinds of additions made to stories about the women in the Buddha's life would surely be labeled "feminist" were they to be suggested today because of the ways in which they expand and elevate the status and accomplishments of both Yasodhara and Prajapati.

Yasodhara

The story of Yasodhara (Sanskrit: Yashodhara) has been greatly elaborated both in ways that expand on the more familiar story of how Siddhartha left her and her newborn infant and in ways that depart radically from that story. Stories that expand on the more familiar narrative magnify her grief, portraying her as severely reproaching her former husband when she finally sees him again, and also magnify the importance of her role as the wife and companion of the future Buddha, life after life. These narratives emphasize the importance of her long partnership with the future Buddha, and her unfailing, constant loyalty to him, in his development of the merit and virtue required for the bodhisattva to achieve enlightenment. But these same texts also go on to narrate Yasodhara's own spiritual achievements, her own enlightenment, parinirvana, and miraculous powers.

However, the story of Yasodhara is taken in a completely different direction by the Sanskrit *Mulasarvastivada Vinaya*, the vinaya followed by Tibetan Buddhists.[10] In this story, rather than being born the night that Siddhartha abandons his home and family, Rahula, the Buddha's son, is conceived on that night. Yasodhara has frightening dreams after they make love and she experiences great foreboding. She asks Siddhartha only to take her with him wherever he may go, which he promises to do. However, when she wakes up in the morning, he is gone and she is pregnant. Their journey together continues, however, as he struggles toward realization and she remains pregnant for the six years between Siddhartha's departure and his enlightenment. She finally gives birth to their son the same night that he becomes enlightened.

What can one make of this strange story? While it is difficult to regard giving birth and attaining enlightenment as equally significant or outstanding events, because the one is so common and the other so rare, this story obviously tries to maintain a bond between Siddhartha and Yasodhara even after he abandons her. This story emphasizes that even though they were separated, their lives proceeded on the same track: when he fasted, she also fasted; when he began to eat, so did she. Finally her pregnancy and his spiritual quest both reached their climaxes at the same time. While, as a Buddhist woman and a feminist, I do not find anything for me to emulate in this version of Yasodhara's story, I do appreciate the interest in what happened to her after Siddhartha disappeared from her life. One could also read this story as an unsatisfactory attempt to elucidate some enduring and essential partnership between male and female, despite so much emphasis on celibacy in Buddhist tradition, and no matter what the superficial appearances of the story may lead one to believe. Or perhaps one could interpret the story in an even more radical way. Women who become pregnant and give birth are just as valuable as men who renounce the world and become enlightened and should not be so easily dismissed in Buddhism's overall value system. Many women who have gone through pregnancy and childbirth, something no man has ever experienced, probably *do* feel that their accomplishment is as difficult and important as anything any man could do, whatever Buddhist monks might think. It is not difficult to imagine that such thoughts motivated the authors of this curious narrative.

Later Thai stories elaborate on Yasodhara's extreme grief and sense of injustice at being abandoned even though she had served her husband well.[11] These episodes are inserted into narratives about the Buddha's first visit to his hometown after his enlightenment experience. Bimba, as Yasodhara is called in this narrative, alone among his relatives refused to greet him. Instead, she sobs inconsolably in her room, falling unconscious and repeatedly stating that her terrible fate must be the result of bad karma from previous lives. Finally, she sees the Buddha, unloosens her long hair, and sweeps it over his feet. She pays her respects to him and reproaches him: "Oh my lord, I pay my respects to you. I am unlucky and ashamed before you. You abandoned me and our child without any compassion. . . . You never gave me any indication that you would leave me alone for such a long time."[12] Her extreme grief would not be considered exemplary behavior by many Buddhists, but it certainly mirrors how many women feel about this narrative. It can be a relatively difficult story to "explain away." It is quite refreshing to learn that a radical criticism of the Buddha's behavior could be inserted into narratives about his life long after Buddhism became the dominant religion of Thailand.

Sinhalese literature from the Theravada tradition, translated by Ranjini Obeyesekere in 2009, follows the more familiar narrative of Yasodhara from early Pali and Sanskrit traditions but takes it in a completely different direction.[13] Of the two texts in question, the *Yasodharapadanaya* ("The Sacred Biography of Yasodhara") dates from the twelfth or thirteenth century, while the other, the

Yasodharavata ("The Story of Yasodhara"), is a folk poem with no certain dates or authors. Both texts have roughly the same story line, ending with Yasodhara's triumphant parinirvana as a miracle-working arhat who is highly praised by the Buddha. Both also treat Siddhartha's abandonment of Yasodhara and her reaction to it, and both also recount the long partnership between Siddhartha and Yasodhara. It was said that their partnership began when the future Siddhartha/Buddha first took his bodhisattva vow; the future Yasodhara vowed in that earlier life always to be reborn as Siddhartha's partner and always to support him. One part of her story thus emphasizes her loyalty and the many ways in which she helped the Bodhisattva along on his path.

The folk poem, *The Story of Yasodhara*, focuses mainly on Yasodhara's emotional devastation at being abandoned by Siddhartha. She reproaches him by recounting how she always supported him in his previous lives, and she voices her main complaint: not that he abandoned her but that he abandoned her without telling her what he was doing, which seems unfair to her given how loyal and helpful she has been in all their past lives. In this literature, a voice is given to the faithful but abandoned wife, of whom there probably have been many throughout Buddhist history. In such literature, a figure who probably was almost never listened to or given any real importance or credence in life, as opposed to literature, can express her sorrow and frustration. It is easy to imagine ordinary women identifying with this literary figure and finding solace for their own sorrows about unfulfilling or unfulfilled relationships. Obeyesekere, the poem's translator, notes that women still sing these laments as they work, improvising new verses as they labor.[14] Such literature is clearly untouched by any connection with Western feminism. Yet it demonstrates what many current Western feminists would regard as a feminist agenda: giving voice to otherwise silenced women, exploring their emotional lives, and providing them with religious folk heroes with whom they can identity. That it would never occur to many indigenous commentators to link such literature with feminism demonstrates just how slippery and ultimately irrelevant that label can be.

Both texts narrate how Yasodhara became a nun and attained arhatship through her diligent practice, thus focusing on her spiritual life as well as her relationship with the Buddha. In both works, Yasodhara, now an aged arhat nun, enters parinirvana and is praised by the Buddha, who, in the folk poem, places flowers on her bier.[15] However, *The Sacred Biography of Yasodhara* is completely a narrative about Yasodhara's triumphant parinirvana. At the beginning of the text, Yasodhara decides it is time to enter parinirvana and she goes to declare this to the Buddha. The Buddha then makes the following statement about her:

> This revered person is one who has the knowledge to see uncountable eons of past lives. She has acquired the Divine Eye and Divine Ears and has the unique and special powers of sight and hearing. She has extinguished all Defilements. She has arrived at the summit of the Three Kinds of Knowledge. She has supernormal powers not second to the Buddha.[16]

The Buddha then asks her to demonstrate her supernormal powers, and she puts on a show of miracles that, were someone to try to create a film version of the narrative, would require extremely talented masters of special effects. After that, a long description of how much Yasodhara helped Siddhartha throughout their various lives is inserted into the narrative about her parinirvana. In contrast to the folk poem, in this more orthodox and literary text, her grief at being abandoned is not mentioned. Rather, as she recounts their lives together, Yasodhara proclaims that no matter what Siddhartha had done to her in previous existences, she always accepted his behavior and supported him. Then the Buddha takes the stage again to speak himself of how great Yasodhara is, declaring that, together with him, she had practiced all the virtues required for enlightenment herself. At the end of her display of miracles, her recounting of her loyalty and helpfulness to the Buddha throughout all their samsaric lives together, and his extravagant praises of her as having attained superlative states of spiritual development, she goes back to her nunnery and attains parinirvana that night. In this text also, elaborate funeral rites are performed and the Buddha himself takes her relics, has a stupa constructed over them, and offers flowers and incense.[17]

These stories are almost equally focused on the partnership between the Buddha and Yasodhara and on Yasodhara's merits as a practitioner in her own right. Like the curious story in the *Mulasarvastivada Vinaya*, these texts seem unwilling to focus almost solely on the Buddha while ignoring Yasodhara. Though, of course, she could not be portrayed as equally important with the Buddha, these texts are much more interested in the intensity of their partnership and how it contributed to the whole endeavor of the Buddha's long journey. It is almost as if the always-male future Buddha is declared to be incomplete and inadequate without a feminine counterpart, whereas in more conventional and more familiar stories, the focus in entirely on the male Buddha, and Yasodhara is very much an afterthought who disappears from the story as soon as Siddhartha leaves his palace. (Given Indian society of the day, he would have had to have a wife while he lived as a householder, but she doesn't need to play any significant role in his life.) But in these stories, their relationship continues "until death did them part," and Yasodhara is essential to the overall story line. Though many male-dominant elements remain in these texts—such as that Yasodhara accepts abuse from her partner and yet remains loyal to him—nevertheless, the interest in her side of the partnership, and indeed the emphasis on the partnership quality of their long relationship, are quasi-"feminist" elements, especially when compared to the more usual dismissal of Yasodhara.

Even more "feminist" is the insistence that by the end of her life, Yasodhara had fully completed the path to arhatship and had attained miraculous powers "not second to the Buddha." Whatever she had gone through or endured previously, by the end of her life, she was no longer inferior to the Buddha except in the way that all other enlightened beings are "inferior" to the Buddha— they could not discover the path to nirvana unaided. But once she attained realization, her freedom was just as real and complete as that of the Buddha. How different from the earlier, more conventional accounts and how much more "feminist" that her story would end with her arhatship rather than ending when Siddhartha walked out of their house without her. And how "feminist" that the Buddha himself honors her relics. Surely this story is important to women reared in a tradition that often taught them that women could not attain enlightenment.

Mahapajapati

The stories eventually told about Pajapati (Sanskrit: Prajapati), the Buddha's foster mother and the first nun—also known as Gotami (Pali) or Gautami (Sanskrit)—are even more impressive as "feminist" additions to the standard stories about her that circulate, though in a sense they are less elaborate. Yasodhara's story has emotional resonance because of her long partnership with Siddhartha as his wife and companion, life after life, whereas it was not thought that Mahapajapati had a complicated emotional relationship with Siddhartha even in her last life, let alone life after life. Rather, her previous life stories tell of how, in an earlier life, she was born during the life of Buddha Padumuttara and watched as that Buddha made his aunt the chief of all the nuns. She resolved to be that same woman in the lifetime of a future Buddha. After that she was reborn as a goddess in the Heaven of the Thirty-Three and lived there for a long time. The rest of her lives are passed over quickly until she is reborn in her final life as Siddhartha's aunt.[18]

Her story is told in the *Apadana* section of the fifth nikaya (the *Khuddaka Nikaya*), usually thought to be the latest collection of texts included in the sutta section of the Pali Canon, so this literature is much older than the Sinhalese texts about Yasodhara. The *Apadana* consists of stories of the previous lives of famous monks and nuns who had lived and attained nirvana during the lifetime of the historical Buddha. It is thought that they were composed in the immediate post-Ashokan era (the last two centuries B.C.E.) when Buddhism was rapidly becoming a popular religion. It has been suggested that these previous life stories were inspirational for the many laypeople now becoming Buddhists who would not become monks or nuns in their present lives but could model their lives on the stories of how famous monks and nuns had lived in their earlier lives.[19] This text has been ably translated and commented on by Jonathan S. Walters.[20]

Like the Sinhalese texts about Yasodhara, this text is fundamentally an account of Mahapajapati's parinirvana. At the beginning of the text, Mahapajapati, being old and not wishing to experience the demise of the Buddha, decides that she should die—reach parinirvana—first. She goes to the Buddha to see him one last time and tell him of her decision. The text ends with a description of the funeral rites for Mahapajapati and her five hundred nuns who also "went out" with her, followed by extravagant praise of her by the Buddha. Inserted into this narrative is much advice to other Buddhists, given by both Mahapajapati and the Buddha, accounts of Mahapajapati's earlier lives, and an account of the final conversation between the Buddha and Mahapajapati. In this context, only a few episodes relevant to the topic of indigenous "feminism" or proto-feminism can be discussed.

In a brief, interesting conversation, obviously referring to the well-known text in which the Buddha is so reluctant to found the nuns' order, Mahapajapati asks the Buddha to forgive her if that was a fault. But then immediately, without waiting for any reply from the Buddha, she proclaims:

> Unforgivable! Forgive!
> Why should I praise my virtue now?
> What more is there to say to you
> When I am going to nirvana?[21]

In another telling verse, she says:

> That state which is not seen by elders
> Nor by non-Buddhist teachers
> Is witnessed by some Buddhist girls
> When they are only seven.[22]

For our topic, however, the most pertinent statement is a request the Buddha makes to Mahapajapati after she tells him that it is time for her to "go out" and that she has achieved the Buddha's teaching. He replies,

> Yet still there are these fools who doubt
> That women too can grasp the truth.
> Gotami, show miracles
> That they might give up their false views.[23]

She complies with his request, putting on a show of miracles at least equal to the one put on by Yasodhara. In addition to telling us that Buddhists had begun to rely too much on miracles as proof for the cogency of the Buddhist teachings, this verse clearly demonstrates that Buddhists had already begun to doubt that women could attain enlightenment, a view that became ever more entrenched in many parts of the Buddhist world. But this text represents the Buddha as saying that this is a "false view." If it is a false view according to the Buddha, how could anyone persist in the belief that women cannot attain enlightenment? What could be a more "feminist" stance than representing the Buddha as correcting the false views of the majority of his followers when they indulge in inaccurate and negative views or practices concerning women? If feminism can be defined as "any movement that deliberately seeks to raise the status of women from an accepted status quo," then clearly the authors of this Buddhist text from the late pre-Christian centuries were indigenous Buddhist "feminists."

The scholar who has most studied the *Apadana* literature, Jonathan S. Walters, goes even further. He claims that in the thought-world of these texts, men were always reborn as men and women as women.[24] If this belief is combined with a belief that women cannot attain enlightenment, a dire problem results. The Buddhist goal of enlightenment and freedom from perpetual rebirth would be completely unavailable to roughly half the human population, including many pious and diligent Buddhist women. Walters sees Gotami's story as an attempt to solve this problem by portraying Gotami as "the female counterpart of the Buddha, the founder and leader of the nuns' order who parallels (though does not supersede)

Gotama, the founder and leader of the monks' order." She is nothing less than "the Buddha for women," he claims.[25] He bolsters this interpretation by emphasizing that in this text, Mahapajapati is always called by her clan name, Gotami, whereas in other literature she is usually called by her given name, Pajapati. The significance of the name is that Gotami is thus portrayed as a female Buddha. "'Gotami' is, grammatically speaking, the exact feminine equivalent of the name Buddha was known by, 'Gotama.'"[26] We may conclude this line of investigation by quoting another verse from the *Apadana*. The text says of Gotami's "going out,"

> The Buddha's great nirvana, good,
> But not as good as this one.
> Gotami's great going out
> Was positively stellar.[27]

We do not have to engage in a competition between Gotama and Gotami to conclude definitely that this text presents a strong argument that women are not inferior to men in their spiritual capabilities. Surely if this text were being written today, some would want to reject it as "feminist" rather than including it in the canon of Buddhist sacred writings!

We can draw two conclusions from these examples of how Buddhists expanded their repertoire of stories about the two women most important in the life of the historical Buddha. The first concerns the *tradition* of Buddhist contestations of gender. To me, this literature is an attempt to elevate the status, both of these two women and of women in general, by adding to the previous narratives about their lives in ways that indicate that, whatever earlier portraits of them may have presented, their realization was not lesser than that of the Buddha or any male arhat. This is consistent with early Buddhist teaching that, although only a Buddha could discover the dharma, after that, anyone could realize it fully, including any woman. It also seems likely that the stories of Pajapati, Yasodhara, and other women were expanded precisely because the status of Buddhist women had begun to decline and some wise

Buddhists could see that such a situation was not in accord with fundamental Buddhist teachings. These stories were a deliberate corrective to an inappropriate, un-dharmic gender hierarchy that had begun to infiltrate Buddhism. Today such a corrective would be labeled "feminism."

The ambiguity and complexity of these newly retold familiar stories make them worth close analysis. The most important point revealed by these developing stories is that male dominance has *always* been contested in Buddhism. A tradition of Buddhist male dominance and patriarchy is certainly more than evident, but it is not the whole story. Contrary to accusations made by both Asians and Westerners, such contestation should not be regarded as a "feminist innovation" or as solely due to Western feminism. I am one of the Western Buddhist feminists looking for relevant female role models in Buddhist scriptures, and I have long regarded this search as important for contemporary Buddhists, whether men or women. Closer study of Buddhist records shows that there are many more relevant female role models than Western Buddhists were aware of, at least thirty years ago. However, it is tempting and easy to turn this search for relevant historical role models into a dualistic black-and-white judgment about Buddhism's past, which is both naive and counterproductive. By investigating the ongoing traditions of Buddhist storytelling about these and other women, I suggest that we can rescue a narrative that is both more accurate and more relevant than the common claims either that Buddhism has been unrelievedly patriarchal or that Buddhism does not have any problems regarding gender, making feminist critiques irrelevant.

Thus we return to a basic point: There have always been "feminist" movements in Buddhism. They are "indigenous" to Buddhism. Therefore, labeling a proposed change, such as reinstating the nuns' sangha, as "feminist" and then using that label to dismiss the proposal as obviously Western and colonial, something that indigenous Asian Buddhists would never think up, is an argument unworthy of any serious Buddhist. Is restoring the nuns' sangha a genuinely Buddhist concern that would promote genuinely Buddhist goals? Why the assumption that critiquing Buddhist traditions cannot be done on Buddhist grounds but must stem from some foreign perspective? For example, highlighting the way in which the Buddha emphasizes the importance of the fourfold sangha has become a major argument for reinstating the nuns' sangha. It *is* also an inherited, traditional Buddhist norm, whether or not it has been sufficiently recognized in recent Buddhist history.

I would contend that one does a great disservice to the intelligence and integrity of Buddhists, whether Asian or Western, if one claims that we should passively accept everything that has become traditional without bringing any critical thought to bear on the issues. It is equally problematic to assume that such critical perspectives and values would stem from non-Buddhist rather than Buddhist sources. Insofar as these critical perspectives derive from Buddhist inspiration, they are indigenous to Buddhism, whether uttered by Westerners or by Asians. So let us discuss Buddhism's existing problems with gender equity on the merits of the issues, rather than by resorting to name-calling. It is never appropriate to dismiss a proposal by attaching the label "feminist" to it, unless we want to dismiss much Buddhist teaching.

The second major conclusion takes us back to the relevance of "story" in religious discourse. It is noteworthy that the medium chosen for this message is story rather than discursive, abstract modes of expression. Unless one is too sophisticated and rationalistic, anyone can understand a story and be touched by its power and vividness. I would also claim that if people still live within their sacred stories, they always want to retell the old, traditional sacred stories in new ways that address the contemporary situation. Thus, rather than indicating irreverence or disregard for the tradition, retelling stories and changing them, even changing them drastically, indicates that the values of the tradition still reverberate deeply in people's lives and psyches. If the story can no longer be retold but has ossified into a sacrosanct version that cannot be tampered with, then the story has died and can no longer really inspire people and enliven their lives.

The quest to discover the empirical history surrounding these sacred stories is in no way damaging to them as living scripture, but fundamentalism, the insistence that the sacred story is empirical history, completely deadens it, depriving it of its ability to be a living scripture newly relevant in every age and generation because the story is always being retold, amplified, and updated. If one understands and appreciates what a living scripture is, one understands that there can be no final, definitive version of the sacred story, that it can never really be fully canonized and closed down to new retellings.

Outsiders might ask if such storytelling is still alive and well in Buddhism in the modern era. Certainly, regarding the historical Buddha himself, this storytelling activity continues into the present, especially in the Asian Buddhist world. A popular series of Japanese comic books titled *Buddha*, drawn by Osamu Tezuka and portraying the life of the Buddha, ran from September 1972 to December 1983,[28] and a lavishly produced, ongoing Indian Bollywood-style TV series on his life—titled *Buddhaa: Rajaon Ka Raja* ("Buddha: The King of Kings")—began airing in 2013. Thich Nhat Hahn's long, novel-like "biography" of the Buddha[29] blends traditional stories with modern concerns such as social equality and the status of women and is popular among Western students of Buddhism. A delightful "children's book" version of the Buddha's life, *The Cat Who Went to Heaven*,[30] is set in Japan. One can see storytelling continuing in the realm of cinema. A 1993 movie, *Little Buddha*, retells the Buddha's story in a contemporary context, and at the center of the story is the suggestion that a girl might be a *tulku*, a rebirth of an important *male* Buddhist teacher. This suggestion would have been unthinkable in a traditional Tibetan context in which rebirth as a female could only indicate a major lapse on the part of the formerly male teacher, but it does resonate with modern and Western viewers unsatisfied with conventional male dominance. Although the Dalai Lama has suggested that *if* his incarnation lineage continues, there could well be a future female Dalai Lama, I suspect that suggestion is more positively received by Westerners than by Tibetans.

SIX

MY AUDIENCE
AND PURPOSE

Whom am I hoping to influence with this book? As a Western Buddhist scholar-practitioner, I first direct my comments to Western Buddhists. I hope that my comments contribute to the development of Western Buddhism as a Buddhism that is free of the patriarchies that dominate both Western culture and Buddhist religions historically. That is my primary aim and my primary audience. What about Asian Buddhisms? Buddhism, after all, developed in Asia, and many, many more Buddhists live in Asia than in the West. I hope that some of them find my comments interesting or relevant in various ways. Finally, those interested in topics pertaining to gender and religion, or to gender studies more generally, or to socially engaged Buddhists, might also want to consider my comments.

I find myself squeezed between two different sets of audiences, both of whom claim, on differing grounds, that a gender-egalitarian Western Buddhism is not that relevant or important. On the one hand, Asian Buddhists sometimes still try to control Western Buddhisms. Negotiating how to balance the immense gratitude we owe to Asian Buddhists for transmitting Buddhist traditions and practices to us with the legitimate needs of Western practitioners to be free of aspects of Asian Buddhism—including gender hierarchies—that just don't work for us can be difficult. It is made especially difficult by the fact that some Asian Buddhists resist the claim that Western ideas or practice could have any relevance for them. At the same time, many social activists in the West and many engaged Buddhists worldwide regard gender oppression as a minor problem that can be solved "later," if it even needs to be solved at all. It is amazing how many men resent being controlled by other men but nevertheless regard it as unproblematic, even appropriate, for them to control "their" women. Additionally, the tendency of social activists to rank oppressions, claiming that their own is the most oppressive and matters the most, causes great difficulty. Their anger at those who foreground a different oppression can be counterproductive. Many times, feminists have been on the receiving end of such anger.

"FEMINISM" AND BUDDHISMS: WESTERN OR ASIAN

Western Buddhist-feminist scholar-practitioners are unrelenting in our fervor to develop a Buddhism that is free of both Western and Buddhist androcentrism, male dominance, and misogyny. That practice has a complex genesis. Because we were socialized in Western cultures, of course there is an inescapable Western imprint on our thinking. Dissatisfaction with what we had inherited as Westerners led us to become Buddhists. Part of that dissatisfaction with our Western inheritance included intense distaste for Western androcentrism, male dominance, and misogyny. We carried that distaste into our Buddhist allegiance. It is not to be expected that we would react any more favorably to Buddhist male dominance than we had to Western male dominance. And it would be hard to deny that Asian Buddhisms exhibit significant male dominance. Nevertheless, some Asian Buddhists dislike it when Western Buddhists critique Buddhist male dominance. It seems to me that they often do not recognize how much our critique of male dominance is a critique of male dominance *altogether*, whether Buddhist or Western. It also seems to me that these Asian Buddhists are not fully aware of how intense and oppressive *Western* male dominance has been.

In fact, in my own case, I resisted my comfort in Buddhist practices and teachings because, as a scholar of comparative studies in religion who had already done major work on gender and religion, I was more than aware of Asian Buddhist patriarchy. But what I saw of nascent Western Buddhisms, already affected by second-wave feminism in the mid- to late 1970s, seemed different.

Had what I saw of early Western Buddhism exhibited the same kind of male dominance I had already experienced in Western religions and knew all too well to be likewise the case in Asian Buddhisms, I would never have signed on. But it did not. Finally, I decided that the "dharma is too profound to let the patriarchs have it all to themselves," as I've often put that decision in shorthand. I never had romantic illusions about Buddhism as the perfect foil to all the problems of Western religions, and I knew the day I took refuge in the Three Jewels that eventually I would have to write *Buddhism after Patriarchy*.

Sorting out what is Buddhist and what is Western in the resulting Buddhist feminism is impossible, as is to be expected for Western Buddhisms altogether. Nevertheless, such boundary-crossing invites potshots from all sides. In the early years, both my colleagues in the feminist theological movement and my Western Buddhist coreligionists thought I had gone crazy. My feminist colleagues could not understand why anyone would join a patriarchal religion, though they understood perfectly why they were trying to make Judaism or Christianity workable for themselves. They apparently could not understand that the *spiritual* practices and teachings of Western religions no longer made sense to me, so working to transform those religions in a feminist direction had become meaningless to me.

My Western Buddhist coreligionists, who had been involved with Buddhism only slightly longer than I had, but who did not have my scholar's knowledge of Asian Buddhist texts and contemporary practices, insisted that, because they had never encountered any Buddhist male dominance, therefore it did not exist. They claimed I was "genderizing the dharma," a heinous offense that should disallow me from ever teaching or publishing anything about Buddhism. It reminds one of eighteen-year-old college freshman girls (term used deliberately) who insist that because they have never experienced sexism in their short, sheltered lives, there is no need for a women's movement.

Then there are certain Western social scientists who study Asian cultures but do not themselves seem to be Buddhist practitioners.

But political correctness is of overriding importance to them. They claim that Westerners who get involved in Buddhism and attempt to influence the development of Buddhist institutions are colonialists stealing other people's spirituality. That claim reveals profound ignorance about Buddhism. Already during the Buddha's lifetime, he reportedly commissioned his disciples to spread his teachings beyond the local area in which he taught. From that beginning, Buddhism spread throughout the world as known by premodern Asians. Why would that spread be expected to stop at the boundaries of the geographic and cultural West?

The interpenetration of Western and Asian Buddhisms is far more complex and important. Though Asian Buddhists often become defensive about Buddhist male dominance, especially when Westerners point it out, it is impossible to deny the fact that Asian Buddhist institutions are male dominated. It was Asians, after all, who came up with the view that the indignities suffered by women under male dominance could be overcome by their future rebirth as men—if they didn't cause any trouble in their current lives as females, which, of course, means not objecting to male dominance, among other things! So the reward for women would be an ability to dominate other women when they become men in their future lives! How could one expect that women who have developed some intellectual and spiritual independence would not find such teachings offensive? Their cultural origins are irrelevant to their offensiveness. They would be equally offensive if they derived from a Western source, and we are as vigilant about Western patriarchy as about any other.

At the same time, it has become clearer in the last thirty years of Buddhist studies in the West that *Western* scholarly androcentrism has clouded what Westerners, including Western practitioners, see when they look at Buddhism. Androcentrism was first described by Simone de Beauvoir in her ground-breaking book *The Second Sex* (1949) and became important in early second-wave feminist scholarship. Androcentrism is, first, a model of humanity that *resides in the scholar's head, not out there* in the so-called data. This model of humanity sees men as ideal, normal human beings, to the extent that women do not have to be specifically mentioned or studied because they are included in a generic "mankind."[1] One should just understand that the term "men" includes women, except when it does not, as in "the men's room." That model of humanity is then imposed on "the data" and greatly distorts the resulting picture.[2] This model of humanity erases women from the picture far more effectively and extensively than does Buddhist patriarchy, which at least acknowledges that male dominance exists and is so unpleasant for women that it needs to be redressed in a future life. I used to joke that the androcentrism of Western scholarship was so pronounced at the beginning of second-wave feminism that a researcher from another galaxy who did not know that human beings come in two sexes would not be able to figure that out from the books these scholars wrote. Only "mankind," all of whose members are addressed as "he," would be found in those books. This mindset has clearly affected Western scholars of Buddhism as well.

Androcentrism was so pervasive in Western scholarship that when I was a graduate student, my mentors insisted there was no need to study women specifically. They were already covered and included in the "generic masculine," it was claimed. This despite obvious gender-role differentiation in all known societies! How could such an absurd claim have scholarly merit? Yet I came close to being kicked out of graduate school at the University of Chicago for demonstrating that androcentric scholarly assumptions simply could not and did not "cover and include" data about women's religious lives at all, let alone adequately or completely! Regarding Buddhism, by highlighting some facts and ignoring others, Western scholars have, in fact, created a portrait of Buddhism that, in some cases, is more male dominant than the data warrant. Examples of such misrepresentation were presented in chapter 5 of this book.

Nevertheless, many Asian Buddhists seem to be allergic to the term "feminism" and are unwilling to investigate what feminism actually is, apart from media stereotypes stemming from the West. For example, a colleague of mine, a Christian theologian, told me about coteaching a course on Buddhist-Christian interchange at a college somewhere in the Pacific Northwest with a Tibetan who had a fancy Tibetan title, either *lama* or *geshe*. One of the topics to be covered was gender, and my Christian colleague suggested, not too surprisingly, that the students be assigned parts of *Buddhism after Patriarchy* for the Buddhist readings on gender. His Tibetan colleague refused the assignment, declining even to read the book on the justification that the subtitle contained the term "feminist"! My Christian colleague pointed out, to no avail, that I am a Buddhist scholar-practitioner, not a non-Buddhist Buddhalogist, and that I also had a Tibetan title (*lopon/acharya*), given to me by my Tibetan teacher. The Christian colleague had to teach the materials on Buddhism and gender himself, despite knowing little about Buddhism. Yet Western students of Tibetan Buddhism are expected to respect Tibetan teachers who have fancy titles unreservedly and uncritically!

Probably it is wiser to set aside the polemical term "feminism" in favor of discussing the actual ideas and practices involved. In many contexts, using the term "feminism" constitutes little more than name-calling. In any case, feminism should never be understood as an angry, anti-men stance. Such emotions are not part of any cogent form of feminism, and attempts to describe it as such only discredits the movement without actually investigating it. I seldom use the term anymore myself, although I am clear as to what I mean by the term—and when I use it, I only mean what I mean by the term. How others might use the term cannot legitimately be imputed onto me or my work. For many years, I have consistently defined feminism simply as "freedom from the prison of gender roles," a definition that includes all sexes and all genders. Sometimes I also use the term in a more limited sense. "Feminism" refers to any movement that deliberately seeks to raise the status of women from an accepted status quo. It is presupposed that such movements result in greater gender equality and equity.

It is difficult to see what could be objectionable about a movement with such goals, unless one asserts that men should control women and women should be socially, economically, and religiously disadvantaged. However, many Asian Buddhists object to "feminism" because they think the movement is "Western" and should be rejected on that ground alone. Several replies to this objection have merit. First, an idea or a practice should not be accepted or rejected on the basis of its source. What should be debated is whether or not it is appropriate for men to control women's lives, not whether feminism is "Western." Second, although I have great sympathy for postmodern perspectives, that sympathy does not extend to claims that all ethics are culturally relative and specific. I cannot assent to the claim that protecting women's rights and dignity is merely a modern Western preference with no overriding validity, or that a value system promoting such practices is morally indistinguishable from a value system that does not promote them (by denying education to girls, for example). I would make that claim even if *local women* supported attempts to restrict education for girls. Third, it would be more useful to distinguish between "modern" and "traditional" practices than between Asian and Western Buddhist practices, because that is the relevant dividing line. The entire world has accepted certain modern innovations and practices, to the point that it makes little sense to label them "Western" anymore. As I said at the beginning of chapter 5, Asian Buddhists who reject feminism because it is Western eagerly adopt cell phones, computers, and other technologies, even though they are equally as "Western" as (actually even more Western than) feminism.

Finally, and most important, it is not at all clear that Buddhist feminisms derive only from Western sources. Although the term "feminism" is not used in Asian Buddhist texts, feminist concepts and practices have been part of Buddhism from its beginnings and throughout its entire history, as I have demonstrated in recent articles[3] and in many parts of this book. This fact about traditional Buddhism has been largely missed by androcentric Western scholars of Buddhism, but it could make a great deal of difference for Asian Buddhists. There is plenty of warrant for Buddhist "feminism" in Buddhist sources themselves. Many motifs that would be labeled "feminist" were someone to propose them today are found in texts written centuries before the emergence of contemporary feminism. Therefore, Buddhist feminism, or whatever we're going to call it, does not depend on Western human rights theory, as is so often claimed. It is not that Western human rights theory and Buddhism are necessarily incompatible, but Buddhist feminism does not depend on Western human rights theories, either. It is easily derived from Buddhist texts whose relevance could be discounted only by denying a significant portion of Asian Buddhism and its heritage. They should make a significant difference to those for whom anything "Western" is objectionable.

Thus, regarding my Asian Buddhist audience, I will say only that I would be pleased if they find something helpful in my writings on gender and Buddhism. What I think might be most useful for them is a deeper understanding of the depths of male dominance and misogyny in Western cultures that Western Buddhists must heal from. That is one reason I have often contrasted egalitarian teachings from Buddhism with their Western counterparts that are more male dominant. If Asian teachers had more understanding of the vastness of Western misogyny and male dominance, they might react more compassionately to their Western students who object to male dominance.

In particular, I hope that they might understand how much their male students need to overcome the views of male superiority that they inherited from their Western cultural upbringing before they can begin to approach the enlightened state beyond gender, neither male nor female. That is necessary if these male students are ever to truly study the self, transcend the prison of gender roles, and live up to the gender neutrality and gender egalitarianism that are so clearly the heart of the Buddhist view.

Likewise, these Asian teachers need to understand more clearly how much Western misogyny and teachings of female defectiveness and inferiority have damaged Western female dharma students. Many of those women need to gain some confidence and overcome low self-esteem before they can approach that enlightened state themselves. Eventually one must absorb the idea that frequent and fervent declarations that enlightened mind is beyond gender, neither male nor female, are incompatible with male dominance, misogyny, and the prison of gender roles.

When Asians become defensive about Western frustration with Buddhist male dominance, they may think we Westerners are speaking from a position of superiority, as if Western cultures have their act together on gender. They do not, any more than do Asian cultures. This is a problem we all have to solve together in various ways. As a somewhat privileged Western woman, I am grateful and thankful that I have attained some freedom from male control. Men do not and cannot control my life. I have been able to receive an education and become economically independent. I have been able to make my own spiritual choices. That is what I want for all women and men, call it what you will: feminism or any other name.

What Asians make of these suggestions is not for me but for Asian Buddhists to decide. Just as I insist that Asian Buddhists should not try to control Western Buddhists who do not want to adopt Asian Buddhist practices of male dominance, so the elimination of male-dominant practices in Asian Buddhisms has to be an Asian project. Because Western and Asian societies still differ, male dominance or clinging to gender identity can manifest differently in the two regions. Nonetheless, I still find it difficult to imagine how clinging to gender identity could ever be justified on Buddhist grounds. I also find it difficult to imagine how one could promote or justify male dominance without clinging to an ego based on gender identity. Furthermore, I expect Asian Buddhists not to vilify me, as been done by some, for promoting a more "feminist," which is to say, a more egalitarian, Buddhism in my own culture.

To return, then, to the question of what audience I primarily hope to influence with this book, the answer is unambiguously, and unreservedly, *Western Buddhists*. Obviously, how would I even be able to have much impact on Asian Buddhists? I do not expect Western Buddhists to "rescue" Asian Buddhism, though I have sometimes been misinterpreted as having suggested such a thing. In *Buddhism after Patriarchy*, I did write of the auspicious coincidence of Buddhism and feminism in the West.[4] But those comments were about *Western Buddhists*, not about Asian Buddhists. Asian Buddhist teachers and the second wave of feminism came together in the West in the late 1960s, creating a new situation for Buddhism. Western Buddhism in its current form has two parents—Asian Buddhism and second-wave feminism. It is impossible to imagine that a situation in which about half the Western dharma teachers are women could have developed as it did, within a generation, without the influence of second-wave feminism in the West. The point of comments about the "auspicious coincidence" of Buddhism and feminism in the West is to emphasize that Western Buddhists have no excuse whatsoever for allowing any male dominance to creep into our forms of Buddhism. Buddhist teachings are gender neutral and gender egalitarian, as Asian teachers have so often reminded us when citing that enlightened mind is beyond gender, neither male nor female. That's the sole relevant factor regarding gender for Western Buddhists. Because we are Buddhists, therefore, the deep heritage of Western misogyny, often based in Western religions, is *utterly irrelevant* to us, or at least it should be. Because we are Westerners, the male-dominant forms of cultures that support Asian Buddhist male-dominated institutions in Asia are also irrelevant to us. There is no reason for Western Buddhism not to take a fresh start of freedom from the prison of gender roles. None whatsoever.

What does this mean for Asian Buddhists? It's up to them. If they want more gender-egalitarian Buddhist institutions, they will have to create them. If they choose to retain male-dominated institutions, that's their choice. Based on the sum of my own life experiences, however, as a woman, as a scholar, as a feminist, and as a teacher of dharma to Western Buddhists, I will never be able to understand why people would choose male dominance over freedom from the prison of gender roles.

LIBERATING ONE LIBERATES ALL: WHOSE LIBERATION MATTERS MOST?

This book is written from the perspective of someone who has suffered mainly from one specific version of the prison of gender roles—that of a woman living in male-dominated and extremely misogynist

Western culture as well as a woman dealing to a lesser extent with traditional Buddhist institutions. My specific situation does not mean that I am unmindful of the situations of those dealing with other aspects of the prison of gender roles or with other kinds of cultural deprivations. When I give talks on the prison of gender roles and the various versions of it, especially from a Buddhist perspective, people often ask me, "What about the many other forms of difficulty?" I usually reply that the methods I have used—studying the literature of my tradition, contemplating deeply the basic teachings of my tradition, and speaking up (speaking truth to power)—are easily transferable; and although they are often slow and not as effective as one might prefer, they do work to some extent.

Social activists who are deeply concerned with a specific issue often foreground that issue to the extent that they become competitive about whose cause matters most, whose pain matters the most. Unfortunately, discussions of oppression and liberation sometimes devolve into arguments about whose liberation should come first, whose oppression hurts the most, and even whether certain groups—women, for instance—deserve better living circumstances or liberation at all. These discussions about rights, justice, liberation, and oppression are admittedly more prominent in the West than in Asia or in traditional Asian Buddhism. For Western Buddhists, such language is impossible to avoid; it is part of our Western heritage, though we must be careful to wean ourselves from the ideology and anger that often characterize such language in Western discourse and that are totally inappropriate for Buddhist sensibilities. And notably, through the international engaged Buddhist movement, concern about a just and appropriate social order is becoming increasingly characteristic of Asian Buddhist discussions as well. In our thoroughly interconnected and interdependent world, it makes less and less sense to make distinctions about discussions being relevant for Western Buddhists but not Asian Buddhists or vice versa.

Women often land on the underside of polarized discussions about whose liberation should come first or whose oppression hurts more. In liberation movements, it is common for men to care intensely about their own liberation from domination by other men—men of other races, cultures, or nation-states—but to see nothing problematic at all about wanting to control "their" women. But can it ever be appropriate for men to own women, as the term "their" women would indicate? Reflect on how easily such language about "their" or "our" women rolls off the tongues of many, without seeming at all problematic to them or to their audiences. Such unconscious language about gender is extremely revealing. That is why using language more precisely, in gender-neutral and gender-inclusive ways, is so important for Buddhist feminists who advocate for such language in Buddhist liturgies—often to be ridiculed and dismissed by male fellow practitioners, and even sometimes by women.

Second-wave feminism began when women involved in the civil rights and peace movements of the 1960s became fed up with having roles that were limited to making coffee and running the copy machines for the men who were directing these movements. In fact, in 1964, Stokely Carmichael quipped that the only position for women in his radical civil rights organization was "prone."[5] Joke or not, the comment reflects a widespread attitude about women's rights, independence, and dignity, even in movements for social justice, that created legitimate frustrations among women. Then and now, women have been told that their concerns for better treatment within their own societies are trivial compared to "larger concerns," which always means something men want for themselves. These issues are often racialized. "Feminism" should be avoided because it is claimed to involve nothing more than attempts by outsiders to protect brown and black women from brown and black men. Brown and black women should be mainly concerned with helping "their" men rather than their own oppression as women. In a racialized context, such recommendations effectively remove any focus from the reality that, just as white men sometimes abuse or oppress white women, black and brown men sometimes abuse or oppress black and brown women.

Likewise, engaged Buddhist movements, both Asian and Western, often totally ignore women's concerns in favor of rants against the International Monetary Fund, various national governments, and international businesses and the economic or environmental fallout of their practices. For example in the Festschrift collected to celebrate the seventieth birthday of Sulak Sivaraksa, the important Thai engaged-Buddhist leader, only three out of eighty-three articles dealt with gender issues in any way.[6] Conveniently for Buddhists, these criticisms are directly outward, toward institutions that Buddhists don't control themselves. It is easy to be critical of organizations that one does not and cannot control. But Buddhists do control their own institutions and the gender arrangements within them, as they have throughout Buddhist history. Yet Buddhist gender arrangements are no more equitable than those of any other religion or society. Why isn't domestic violence within Buddhist households or the trafficking of Buddhist girls as worthy of denunciation as repressive governments? If gender is discussed in a collection of articles on engaged Buddhism, the only topic discussed is nuns' ordination, as if that were the only issue Buddhist women face. Unfortunately, that, too, boils down to a situation of men controlling women. Men take the prerogative of deciding whether women can receive full ordination in the monastic lineages in which such ordinations are no longer or never were performed. They make this claim even though men's interrupted ordination lineages have been restored on more than one occasion and in spite of the fact that, if anything can be attributed to the historical Buddha, one would have to conclude that he set up a religious community consisting of four types of disciples— laymen, laywomen, monks, and *nuns*.[7]

Unfortunately, especially in America, discussions of differing oppressions and the social movements meant to counteract them often devolve into a "race to the bottom," a claim to be the most victimized of all. I characterize this unfortunate development as a claim that "I am victimer than thou and, therefore, thee owes me! Big time!" In Buddhist terms, the victim ego is one of the most difficult to work with because it is so tenacious. It justifies so much self-pity and resists healing because of the privilege that can go with being a victim. Insofar as the conventional, worldly ego is concerned, being a victim is a particularly safe haven because it is so difficult to give up this ego style. As long as the victim ego is retained, enlightenment will most definitely be subverted.

Therefore, Buddhist women, Buddhists, women, and all others who care about social justice need to be especially cautious not to fall into playing the victim game, especially in a competitive manner: "We are the most oppressed of all, so we deserve the most consideration." Such claims intensify anger and resentment, both on one's own part and on the part of others. Such emotions do not promote enlightenment. They encourage groups that otherwise could help each other to instead devolve into competitive, mutually resentful camps. That is why politicians love to play "divide and conquer." Unfortunately, they are often successful. The tendency to create competitive hierarchies among human beings seems to be a strong worldly or samsaric habitual tendency, and such competitive claims to victimhood are one of its least useful manifestations. The most successful way to avoid falling into this trap is to foster as much awareness as possible about all oppressed groups rather than to claim uniquely oppressed status for one's own group.

Buddhist wisdom has a practical slogan for dealing with potential difficulties inherent in ranking oppressions: "Liberating one liberates all." This principle is first articulated, at least to my knowledge, in the *Sandhinirmocana Sutra*, a difficult Mahayana sutra usually classified as belonging to the "third turning," the "final" set of sutra teachings, at least according to some schools of Buddhism. As translated by John Powers, the relevant passage reads:

> monks who practice yoga, having completely realized the such-ness of one aggregate, the selflessness of the phenomena that is the ultimate, do not have to seek further for suchness, for the ultimate, and for selflessness in each of the other aggregates, or in the constituents. . . .[8]

In other words, once you really "get" something definitively, once you truly understand one thing, you understand every other thing of the same type equally thoroughly. One does not have repeat the process of investigation and contemplation that led to the initial breakthrough with every other similar phenomenon. One can safely assume that the insight holds generally.

Applied to the potential for a competitive race to be the most oppressed, the "victimest of all," this principle would mean that there is no need to question the relevance of work that has already been done regarding one set of oppressions to a different kind of oppression. For example, analysis done on gender could be transferable to issues of race or sexual orientation and vice versa. Therefore, someone whose primary issue involves race or sexual orientation should not regard someone who has worked primarily on gender issues with hostility or claim that their work is inadequate because it does not usually directly address race, gender identity, or sexual orientation. Unfortunately, such bitter and hostile accusations between members of these various communities are relatively common. For example, while giving a talk on gender issues, I have been bitterly attacked because I don't usually address issues of sexual orientation. But why the assumption that unless I directly address an endless list of social woes, I must be ignorant of or hostile to those affected by other kinds of oppression? There are practical limitations to how much time and energy one can put into the many causes and issues that are all worthy. It is egocentric to expect everyone who cares about greater equity in society to put *my* issue first. If Buddhists understand Buddhist teachings, they should not fall into this trap.

What if this principle that "liberating one liberates all" doesn't seem to be working? What if someone who is recognized as having deeply penetrated Buddhist teachings still engages in or promotes inappropriate relative practices? Such questions often surface, for example when revered teachers engage in sexual relationships with students that seem ethically questionable. What if a Buddhist teacher were to display racism or homophobia? When it was revealed that revered Japanese Zen Buddhist leaders promoted Japanese militarism and imperialism before World War II, their Western disciples were deeply troubled.

It could be argued that even the Buddha, at least as represented in some Buddhist texts, seemed to favor male dominance. Difficult as it may be for students to accept, trustworthy insight into ultimate truth doesn't necessarily translate into faultless understanding of contemporary social issues. Such limits do not discredit the reliability of the teacher as a dharma teacher, even though students might have to do their own thinking regarding some relative practices and issues. It is unrealistic to expect dharma teachers to be perfect role models in every regard or to be able to guide students in matters about which they may have little understanding themselves.[9] Such discoveries have been disheartening for Western students. But it is unrealistic and overly romantic to expect Buddhist teachers and Buddhism itself to be free of the general faults of religions.

Regarding the question of whose liberation matters most, the acme of Buddhist wisdom is that one is ultimately responsible for one's own state of mind and cannot blame it on others. This can be a steep and unwelcome truth, but it seems incontrovertible. Buddhist nontheism teaches us that no one else is going to liberate us. We are each responsible for our own liberation. Thus, self-liberation first is most important because without self-liberation true compassion, the fuel to work toward the liberation of others, will not develop properly. This is another meaning of the slogan "liberating one liberates all." The more fully one has liberated oneself, the more other instances of social pain will be important. We won't ask whose pain matters the most, and we will see more deeply into what might be helpful in liberating others.

NOTES

INTRODUCTION

1. Nancy Falk, "Rita as Colleague and Collaborator," *Journal of Buddhist-Christian Studies* 31 (2011): 66.
2. Rosemary Reuther, "Rita Gross as Pioneer in the Study of Women and Religion," *Journal of Buddhist-Christian Studies* 31 (2011): 75–78.
3. Rita Gross, "I Am Speechless: Thank You, Colleague Friends," *Journal of Buddhist-Christian Studies* 31 (2011): 93.
4. Rita Gross, "Being a North American Buddhist Woman," in Rita Gross, *A Garland of Feminist Reflections: Forty Years of Religious Exploration* (Berkeley: University of California Press, 2009), 313.
5. Carol L. Flinders, *At the Root of This Longing: Reconciling a Spiritual Hunger and a Feminist Thirst* (San Francisco: HarperOne, 1999).
6. Falk, "Rita as Colleague and Collaborator," 66.
7. Rita Gross, *Buddhism after Patriarchy: A Feminist History, Analysis, and Reconstruction of Buddhism* (Albany: State University of New York Press, 1993), 134–35.
8. Ibid., 3.
9. Ibid., 4, 17–28.
10. Rita Gross, *A Garland of Feminist Reflections: Forty Years of Religious Exploration* (Berkeley: University of California Press, 2009).
11. Ibid., 4.
12. Ibid., 14.
13. Gross, "I Am Speechless," 93.

CHAPTER ONE | Buddhism as Studying the Self and Forgetting the Self

1. Dogen, *Treasury of the True Dharma Eye: Zen Master Dogen's "Shobo Genzo,"* ed. Kazuaki Tanahashi (Boston: Shambhala Publications, 2012), 30.

2. In Buddhism the five skandhas are the five aggregates that comprise a sentient being. These five are form, sensations, perceptions, mental activity, and consciousness. By analyzing each aggregate, one discovers that there is no self that one can cling to. The ayatanas are the six sense organs and the objects of the six senses. (Mind is the sixth sense.) Suffering arises from sensations resulting from contact with the senses. Insight into this process can help end suffering. The dhatus include the ayatanas but also add the element of consciousness for each sense organ (eye-consciousness, ear-consciousness, mind-consciousness, and so forth). The twelve nidanas are also known as the links of dependent origination or dependent arising. They perpetuate the cycle of suffering and rebirth. If analyzed, the cycle can be broken, leading to an end of suffering. The twelve links are ignorance, formation, consciousness, name-and-form, the sense faculties, contact, sensation, craving, grasping, becoming, rebirth, and old age and death.

3. From "Setting in Motion the Wheel of the Dhamma," *Samyutta Nikaya* 56.11.1, in *The Connected Discourses of the Buddha: A Translation of the Samyutta Nikaya*, trans. Bhikkhu Bodhi (Boston: Wisdom Publications, 2000), 1844.

4. Rita Gross, "How Clinging to Gender Subverts Enlightenment," in *Sati Journal*, vol. 2, *Women's Contributions to Buddhism: Selected Perspectives*, ed. Nona Olivia (Redwood City, CA: Sati Center for Buddhist Studies, 2014), 7–14. First published in *Inquiring Mind* 27, no. 1 (fall 2010), 18–19, 32.

CHAPTER TWO | Identity, Egolessness, and Enlightenment

1. The other three are craving for sense pleasures, relying on familiar rituals and rules to save us, and believing that our ideologies and beliefs are absolutely true and correct.

2. See my early 1980 article and the latest version titled "The Clarity in the Anger" in *Garland*, 235–44.

CHAPTER THREE | The Prison of Gender Roles

1. Cathy Newman, "Dalai Lama: I Would Be Pleased If My Successor Was Female," *Telegraph*, April 23, 2013. http://www .telegraph.co.uk/women/womens-life/10010928/Dalai-Lama -I-would-be-pleased-if-my-successor-was-female.html.

2. This list, which is persistent in Buddhist understandings, goes back to the Pali nikayas. It is found in *Samyutta Nikaya* 4.37.3, *Connected Discourses*, Bodhi, 1287.

3. See my essay "Buddhist Women and Teaching Authority," in *Garland*, 281–90.

4. For a related perspective, see Julia O'Faolain and Lauro Martines, eds., *Not in God's Image: Women in History from the Greeks to the Victorians* (New York: Harper and Row, 1973).

5. Gene Reeves, trans., *The Lotus Sutra* (Boston: Wisdom Publications, 2008), 252–53.

6. Kurtis R. Schaeffer, *Himalayan Hermitess: The Life of a Tibetan Buddhist Nun* (Oxford: Oxford University Press, 2004).

7. For my analysis of the text, see "A Relevant Role Model: An Ordinary Woman Who Became Enlightened," in *Eminent Buddhist Women*, edited by Karma Lekshe Tsomo (Albany: State University of New York Press, 2014), 229–40.

8. Schaeffer, *Himalayan Hermitess*, 142.

9. Kim Gutschow, *Being a Buddhist Nun: The Struggle for Enlightenment in the Himalayas* (Cambridge, MA: Harvard University Press, 2004).

10. Ibid., 17.

11. "'Out of Order' at the Court: O'Connor on Being the First Female Justice," *NPR: Fresh Air*, March 5, 2013. http://www .npr.org/2013/03/05/172982275/out-of-order-at-the-court -oconnor-on-being-the-first-female-justice.

12. I am referring to an ad for canned green beans that features a woman riding a bicycle in a relatively short skirt (https://www .ispot.tv/ad/775S/del-monte-green-beans-song-by-barry -louis-polisar). The camera focuses on her thighs as she rides through the green countryside, then switches to her smiling face. What do canned green beans have to do with women's thighs?

13. Alice Collett, "Pali *Vinaya*: Reconceptualizing Female Sexuality in Early Buddhism," in *Women in Early Indian Buddhism: Comparative Textual Studies*, edited by Alice Collett (Oxford: Oxford University Press, 2013), 62–79.

14. Pascale Engelmajer, *Women in Pali Buddhism: Walking the Spiritual Paths in Mutual Dependence* (New York: Routledge, 2015), 83–86.

15. William Pruitt, trans. *The Commentary on the Verses of the Therīs: Therīgāthā-Aṭṭhakathā Paramatthadīpanī V* (Oxford: Pali Text Society, 1998), 222–32. For the most recent translation of the *Therigatha* verses see Charles Hallisey, trans., *Therigatha: Poems of the First Buddhist Women* (Cambridge, MA: Harvard University Press, 2015), 111–15.

16. Tsultrim Allione, *Women of Wisdom* (London: Routledge and Kegan Paul, 1984), 77.

17. *Karaniya Metta Sutta: The Buddha's Words on Loving-Kindness* (Sn 1.8), translated from Pali by the Amaravati Sangha, Chanting Book Volume One: Morning and Evening Chanting (Pūja) and Reflections (Amaravati Publications, 2015). http://www.accesstoinsight.org/tipitaka/kn/snp/snp.1.08.amar.html. Used by permission.

18. For examples, see Gross, *Buddhism after Patriarchy*, 233.

19. Alan Weisman, *Countdown: Our Last, Best Hope for a Future on Earth?* (New York: Little, Brown, 2013), 91–94.

20. Ibid., 43–47.

21. Ibid., 415.

22. Mohr and Tsedroen, *Dignity and Discipline*, 253.

23. Dorothy Dinnerstein, *The Mermaid and the Minotaur* (San Francisco: Harper and Row, 1978), 150.

24. Ibid., 152.

25. Engelmajer, *Women in Pali Buddhism*, 56–57.

26. "The Book of the Twos," Sutta 33, in Bhikkhu Bodhi, trans., *The Numerical Discourses of the Buddha: A Complete Translation of the Anguttara Nikaya* (Boston: Wisdom Publications, 2012), 153.

27. Engelmajer, *Women in Pali Buddhism*, 57.

28. Dzogchen Ponlop, *Mind beyond Death* (Ithaca, NY: Snow Lion, 2006), 137–38.

29. Susan Bordo, *Unbearable Weight: Feminism, Western Culture, and the Body* (Berkeley: University of California Press, 2003), 90. For a more extended discussion of Aristotle's theory, see Cera R. Lawrence, "On the Generation of Animals," by Aristotle," *The Embryo Project Encyclopedia*, October 2, 2010. http://embryo.asu.edu/pages/generation-animals-aristotle.

30. Bordo, *Unbearable Weight*, 89.

CHAPTER FOUR | Freedom from the Prison of Gender Roles

1. This is a reference to one translation of the opening lines of the Kagyu lineage prayer, "Revulsion is the foot of meditation." In other words, revulsion should not be avoided, because it brings us to see the necessity of being serious about our spiritual path.

2. Bhikkhu Bodhi, trans., *The Middle Length Discourses of the Buddha: A Translation of the Majjhima Nikaya* (Boston: Wisdom Publications, 2005), 230–31.

3. Bodhi, *Connected Discourses*, 877.

4. *Aggañña Sutta* 27.16., in Maurice Walshe, *The Long Discourses of the Buddha: A Translation of the Digha Nikaya* (Boston: Wisdom Publications, 1995), 411.

5. Simone de Beauvoir first astutely articulated this point in the early feminist classic *The Second Sex*, published in 1949, well before the emergence of modern gender studies; nonetheless, these stereotypical assumptions about hormones are still strong in many segments of folk and popular culture.

6. The nikayas are the main divisions of the collection of sutras in the Pali Canon known as the Sutta Pitaka.

7. Engelmajer, *Women in Pali Buddhism*, 13.

8. "The Book of the Ones," in Bodhi, *Numerical Discourses*, 89–90.

9. Ibid., 90.

10. "The Book of the Tens," Sutta 51, in Bodhi, *Numerical Discourses*, 1039–41.

11. "The Book of the Twos," Sutta 55, section 6 ("People"), in Bodhi, *Numerical Discourses*, 168.

12. Collett, "Pali *Vinaya*," 63.

13. "The Book of the Fives," Sutta 55, section 5 ("Hindrances"), in Bodhi, *Numerical Discourses*, 683.

14. Bhikkhu Analayo, "*Anguttara-nikaya/Ekottarika-agama*: Outstanding *Bhikkhunis* in the *Ekottarika-agama*," in *Women in Early Indian Buddhism: Comparative Textual Studies*, edited by Alice Collett (Oxford: Oxford University Press, 2013), 97–115.

15. Collett, "Pali *Vinaya*, 65.

16. The other two categories are the sutras (the sermons of the Buddha) and *vinaya* (the teachings for monastics).

17. Bhikkhu Nanamoli, trans., *Vishuddhimagga: The Path of Purifica-tion* (Kandy, Sri Lanka: Buddhist Publication Society, 1991), 447.
18. Gelong Lodro Sangpo, trans., *Abhidharmakosa of Vasubhandu,* vol. 3 (Delhi: Motilal Banarsidass, 2012), 1918–23.
19. Ibid., 2477.
20. Engelmajer, *Women in Pali Buddhism,* 33.
21. Gutschow, *Being a Buddhist Nun,* 17.
22. In the process of thinking about this chapter I reread Betty Frie-dan's 1963 classic study of female unhappiness, *The Feminine Mystique,* in which she coins the phrase "the problem that has no name." The book is an incredibly accurate description of the prison of gender roles—and that prison led to the outburst of second-wave feminism, because of the way in which it forced both women and men into narrow ways of being and deadened women in the process.
23. For more on this notion, see Traleg Kyabgon, *Mind at Ease: Self-Liberation through Mahamudra Meditation* (Boston: Sham-bhala Publications, 2004), 203.

CHAPTER FIVE | Indigenous Buddhist Feminism

1. See my essay "Menstruation and Childbirth as Ritual and Reli-gious Experience among Native Australians," in *Garland,* 131–42.
2. Walshe, *Long Discourses,* 246–47.
3. *Mahaparinibbana Sutta* 3.7–9. Ibid., 247.
4. For the story see *The Kullavagga* 10.1.1–4. In *The Sacred Book of the East,* edited by F. Max Müller, vol. 20 (Oxford: Clarendon Press, 1885), 320–24. Vol. 20 is called Vinaja Texts: Part III, *The Kullavagga,* IV–XII, translated by T. W. Rhys Davids and Her-mann Oldenberg.
5. See Gross, *Buddhism after Patriarchy,* 39.
6. See Thubten Chodron, "A Tibetan Precedent for Multi-tradition Ordination," in Mohr and Tsedroen, *Dignity and Discipline,* 183–94.
7. *Mahaparinibbana Sutta* 5.9., in Walshe, *Long Discourses,* 264.
8. I am embarrassed to concede that I quoted those six lines in *Buddhism after Patriarchy* (44) twenty-five years ago when I was less familiar with Pali literature than I am now. But it does in-dicate how prevalent those six lines were in the anthologies of Buddhist text with which I was working in those days.

9. Bhikkhu Nanamoli, *The Life of the Buddha: According to the Pali Canon* (Kandy, Sri Lanka: Buddhist Publication Society, 1992).

10. See John S. Strong, "A Family Quest: The Buddha, Yasodhara, and Rahula in the *Mulasarvastivada Vinaya*," in Juliane Schober, *Sacred Biography in the Buddhist Traditions of South and Southeast Asia* (Honolulu: University of Hawaii Press, 1997), 113–28. Strong does not attempt to date this material in his article, but the Sarvastivadins and Mulasarvastivadins are among the eighteen schools of early Buddhism. I would suggest that these materials would probably not be earlier than roughly the second century C.E., some seven hundred years into the history of Buddhism.

11. Don Swearer, who translated this episode, took it from a copied manuscript he dated to 1799. See Donald Swearer, "Bimba's Lament," in *Buddhism in Practice*, ed. Donald S. Lopez, Jr. (Princeton, NJ: Princeton University Press, 1995), 541–52.

12. Ibid., 550–51.

13. Ranjani Obeyesekere, trans., *Yasodhara, the Wife of the Bodhisattva: The Sinhala Yasodharavata* ("The Story of Yasodhara") *and the Sinhala Yasodharapadanaya* ("The Sacred Biography of Yasodhara") (Albany: State University Press of New York, 2009).

14. Ibid., 15.

15. Ibid., 55–56.

16. Ibid., 65.

17. Ibid., 79.

18. Jonathan S. Walters, "Gotamī's Story," in Lopez, *Buddhism in Practice*, 128–30.

19. Ibid., 113.

20. Jonathan S. Walters, "A Voice from the Silence: The Buddha's Mother's Story," *History of Religions* 33, no. 4 (May 1994): 350–79.

21. Walters, "Gotamī's Story," 123.

22. Ibid., 125.

23. Ibid., 126.

24. This claim is made by some scholars of Theravada Buddhism. I personally have doubts about whether this claim is correct because it is so contrary to the most elementary Buddhist logic. The fact that *Jataka* and *Apadana* narratives involve sex change from life to life seems to indicate that the impossibility of sex change from life to life was not a fixed doctrine. In later Mahayana

Buddhism, sex change became a common motif in many of the best-known stories.

25. Walters, "Gotamī's Story," 117, and Walters, "A Voice from the Silence," 369–79.
26. Walters, "Gotamī's Story," 117.
27. Ibid., 136.
28. The comics were collected into an eight-volume set and have also been adapted as animated feature-length films. http://www.vertical-inc.com/books/buddha/buddha_top.html.
29. Thich Nhat Hanh, *Old Path, White Clouds: Walking in the Footsteps of the Buddha* (Berkeley, CA: Parallax Press, 1991).
30. Elizabeth Coatsworth and Raoul Vitale, *The Cat Who Went to Heaven* (New York: Aladdin, 2008).

CHAPTER SIX | My Audience and Purpose

1. My own early, classic article on this issue, "Androcentrism and Androgyny in the Methodology of History of Religions," can be found in *Garland,* 55–64.
2. For a summary of my doctoral work demonstrating this thesis, see "Menstruation and Childbirth as Ritual and Religious Experience among Native Americans" in *Garland,* 131–42.
3. "Living Scriptures: The Example of Storytelling about Women Surrounding the Buddha," *Journal of Comparative Scripture* (a bilingual Chinese-English journal), forthcoming, and "Indigenous Non-Western 'Feminism' in Early Buddhist Literature," in *Decolonizing Indian Studies.*, edited by Arvind Sharma (Delhi: D. K. Printworld), 2015.
4. Gross, *Buddhism after Patriarchy,* 215–221.
5. Susan Brownmiller, *In Our Time: Memoir of a Revolution* (New York: Dial, 1999), 14. See excerpt at https://www.nytimes.com/books/first/b/brownmiller-time.html (accessed Dec. 23, 2014).
6. David W. Chappell, ed., *Socially Engaged Spirituality: Essays in Honor of Sulak Sivaraksa on His 70th Birthday* (Bangkok: Sathirakoses-Nagapradipa Foundation, 2003). My essay for that volume, "Why (Engaged) Buddhists Should Care about Gender Issues," can also be found in *Garland,* 245–49.
7. For a full discussion of this movement and these issues, see Thea Mohr and Jampa Tsedroen, eds., *Dignity and Discipline: Reviv-*

ing Full Ordination for Buddhist Nuns (Boston: Wisdom Publications, 2010).

8. John Powers, trans., *Wisdom of Buddha: The Saṁdhinirmocana Sūtra* (Berkeley, CA: Dharma Press, 1995), 61.

9. This issue has been problematic for Western Buddhists, especially regarding certain behaviors engaged in by Asian teachers. For more of my comments on this topic, see the chapter "Helping the Iron Bird Fly: Western Buddhists and Issues of Authority" in my book *Soaring and Settling: Buddhist Perspectives on Contemporary Social and Religious Issues* (New York: Continuum Publishing, 1998), 60–74.

BIBLIOGRAPHY

Allione, Tsultrim. *Women of Wisdom*. London: Routledge and Kegan Paul, 1984.

Amaravati Sangha, trans. *Karaniya Metta Sutta: The Buddha's Words on Loving-Kindness* (Sn 1.8), Chanting Book Volume One: Morning and Evening Chanting (Pūja) and Reflections. Amaravati Publications, 2015. http://www.accesstoinsight.org/tipitaka/kn/snp/snp.1.08.amar.html.

Brownmiller, Susan. *In Our Time: Memoir of a Revolution*. New York: Dial, 1999.

Bodhi, Bhikkhu, trans. *The Connected Discourses of the Buddha: A Translation of the Samyutta Nikaya*. Boston: Wisdom Publications, 2000.

———. *The Middle Length Discourses of the Buddha: A Translation of the Majjhima Nikaya*. Boston: Wisdom Publications, 2005.

———. *The Numerical Discourses of the Buddha: A Complete Translation of the Anguttara Nikaya*. Boston: Wisdom Publications, 2012.

Bordo, Susan. *Unbearable Weight: Feminism, Western Culture, and the Body*. Berkeley: University of California Press, 2003.

Chappell, David W., ed., *Socially Engaged Spirituality: Essays in Honor of Sulak Sivaraksa on His 70th Birthday*. Bangkok: Sathirakoses-Nagapradipa Foundation, 2003.

Coatsworth, Elizabeth and Vitale, Raoul. *The Cat Who Went to Heaven*. New York: Aladdin, 2008.

Collett, Alice, ed. *Women in Early Indian Buddhism: Comparative Textual Studies*. Oxford: Oxford University Press, 2013.

Dinnerstein. Dorothy, *The Mermaid and the Minotaur*. San Francisco: Harper and Row, 1978.

Dogen, *Treasury of the True Dharma Eye: Zen Master Dogen's "Shobo Genzo."* Edited by Kazuaki Tanahashi. Boston: Shambhala Publications, 2012.

Engelmajer, Pascale. *Women in Pali Buddhism: Walking the Spiritual Paths in Mutual Dependence.* New York: Routledge, 2015.

Falk, Nancy. "Rita as Colleague and Collaborator," *Journal of Buddhist-Christian Studies* 31 (2011): 66.

Flinders, Carol L. *At the Root of This Longing: Reconciling a Spiritual Hunger and a Feminist Thirst.* San Francisco: HarperOne, 1999.

Gross, Rita. *Buddhism after Patriarchy: A Feminist History, Analysis, and Reconstruction of Buddhism.* Albany: State University of New York Press, 1993.

———. *A Garland of Feminist Reflections: Forty Years of Religious Exploration.* Berkeley: University of California Press, 2009.

———. "How Clinging to Gender Subverts Enlightenment," *Sati Journal,* vol. 2, *Women's Contributions to Buddhism: Selected Perspectives.* Edited by Nona Olivia. Redwood City, CA: Sati Center for Buddhist Studies, 2014.

———. "I Am Speechless: Thank You, Colleague Friends," *Journal of Buddhist-Christian Studies* 31 (2011): 93.

———. *Soaring and Settling: Buddhist Perspectives on Contemporary Social and Religious Issues.* New York: Continuum Publishing, 1998.

Gutschow, Kim. *Being a Buddhist Nun: The Struggle for Enlightenment in the Himalayas.* Cambridge, MA: Harvard University Press, 2004.

Hallisey, Charles, trans. *Therigatha: Poems of the First Buddhist Women.* Cambridge, MA: Harvard University Press, 2015.

Hanh, Thich Nhat. *Old Path, White Clouds: Walking in the Footsteps of the Buddha.* Berkeley, CA: Parallax Press, 1991.

Kyabgon, Traleg. *Mind at Ease: Self-Liberation through Mahamudra Meditation.* Boston: Shambhala Publications, 2004.

Lawrence, Cera R. "'On the Generation of Animals,' by Aristotle," *The Embryo Project Encyclopedia,* Last modified October 2, 2010. http://embryo.asu.edu/pages/generation-animals-aristotle.

Lopez, Jr., Donald S., ed. *Buddhism in Practice.* Princeton, NJ: Princeton University Press, 1995.

Mohr, Thea and Tsedroen, Jampa, eds. *Dignity and Discipline: Reviving Full Ordination for Buddhist Nuns.* Boston: Wisdom Publications, 2010.

Müller, F. Max. *The Sacred Book of the East.* Oxford: Clarendon Press, 1885.

Nanamoli, Bhikkhu. *The Life of the Buddha: According to the Pali Canon*. Kandy, Sri Lanka: Buddhist Publication Society, 1992.

————, trans., *Vishuddhimagga: The Path of Purification*. Kandy, Sri Lanka: Buddhist Publication Society, 1991.

Newman, Cathy. "Dalai Lama: I Would Be Pleased If My Successor Was Female," *Telegraph*. Last modified April 23, 2013. http://www.telegraph.co.uk/women/womens-life/10010928/Dalai-Lama-I-would-be-pleased-if-my-successor-was-female.html.

Obeyesekere, Ranjani, trans. *Yasodhara, the Wife of the Bodhisattva: The Sinhala Yasodharavata* ("The Story of Yasodhara") *and the Sinhala Yasodharapadanaya* ("The Sacred Biography of Yasodhara"). Albany: State University Press of New York, 2009.

O'Faolain, Julia and Martines, Lauro, eds. *Not in God's Image: Women in History from the Greeks to the Victorians*. New York: Harper and Row, 1973.

"'Out of Order' at the Court: O'Connor on Being the First Female Justice," *NPR: Fresh Air*. Last modified March 5, 2013. http://www.npr.org/2013/03/05/172982275/out-of-order-at-the-court-oconnor-on-being-the-first-female-justice.

Ponlop, Dzogchen. *Mind beyond Death*. Ithaca, NY: Snow Lion, 2006.

Powers, John, trans. *Wisdom of Buddha: The Saṁdhinirmocana Sūtra*. Berkeley, CA: Dharma Press, 1995.

Pruitt, William, trans. *The Commentary on the Verses of the Therīs: Therīgāthā-Aṭṭhakathā Paramatthadīpanī V*. Oxford: Pali Text Society, 1998.

Reeves, Gene. trans. *The Lotus Sutra*. Boston: Wisdom Publications, 2008.

Reuther, Rosemary. "Rita Gross as Pioneer in the Study of Women and Religion," *Journal of Buddhist-Christian Studies* 31 (2011): 75–78.

Sangpo, Gelong Lodro, trans. *Abhidharmakosa of Vasubhandu*, vol. 3. Delhi: Motilal Banarsidass, 2012.

Schaeffer, Kurtis R. *Himalayan Hermitess: The Life of a Tibetan Buddhist Nun*. Oxford: Oxford University Press, 2004.

Schober, Juliane. *Sacred Biography in the Buddhist Traditions of South and Southeast Asia*. Honolulu: University of Hawaii Press, 1997.

Sharma, Arvind, ed. *Decolonizing Indian Studies*. Delhi: D. K. Printworld, 2015.

Tsomo, Karma Lekshe, ed. *Eminent Buddhist Women*. Albany: State University of New York Press, 2014.

University of Chicago Press. *History of Religions* 33, no. 4 (May 1994).

Walshe, Maurice. *The Long Discourses of the Buddha: A Translation of the Digha Nikaya*. Boston: Wisdom Publications, 1995.

Weisman, Alan, *Countdown: Our Last, Best Hope for a Future on Earth?* New York: Little, Brown, 2013.

INDEX